TOMBSTONE WHISPERS:

DEPARTED LEGENDS OF BASEBALL –
THEIR MORAL (AND IMMORAL) LIVES

JOHN A. WOOD

authorHOUSE

AuthorHouse™
1663 Liberty Drive
Bloomington, IN 47403
www.authorhouse.com
Phone: 833-262-8899

Published by AuthorHouse 03/17/2023

ISBN: 979-8-8230-0223-3 (sc)
ISBN: 979-8-8230-0222-6 (e)

Library of Congress Control Number: 2023903652

Print information available on the last page.

This book is printed on acid-free paper.

TABLE OF CONTENTS

ACKNOWLEDGMENTS

Since I have in Appendix II pictures that I took of all of the grave sites (except for two who have no burial sites), I am indebted to Findagrave.com for locating some of them, as well as my debt to Stew Thornley's website that lists the GPS coordinates of all Half of Famers.

Special thanks to those who read all or parts of the manuscript: Baylor colleague Michael Parrish, son Kevin Wood, and former student Ben Simpson. Each made helpful suggestions and corrections.

In 2016, Rowman and Littlefield published my other baseball book, *Beyond the Ballpark: The Honorable, Immoral, and Eccentric Lives of Baseball Legends*. One of their editors, Christen Karniski, edited several chapters included in this current book that had to be cut from *Beyond,* in order to keep the book at a reasonable length.

INTRODUCTION

This book is a follow-up to my 2016 *Beyond the Ballpark: The Honorable, Immoral, and Eccentric Lives of Baseball Legends,* published by Roman and Littlefield. In that book I tried to uncover the character and personality of fifty Hall of Famers. I also noted that I had visited the gravesites of each of them. This new book examines twenty-five men and not all of them are in the Hall of Fame, although several are. Also, there are two who have not been interred: Roy Campanella was cremated and his ashes given to his family, and Ted Williams' body underwent vitrification and is in the Alcor facility in Arizona, where he is joined by his son Ted, and where his daughter Claudia will join them upon her death. I visited the gravesites of the other twenty-three.[1]

I continue to marvel at the accomplishments of ballplayers. Baseball is a unique sport which combines skill and luck in

---

[1] Plus the gravesite of Ray Chapman whose death is described in Appendix I. Special thanks to Stew Thornley whose website provides the exact GPS location of the gravesites (not just the cemetery offices) of all Hall of Famers. The sites of the other players were located in the impressive Findagrave website.

incredible combinations. Anything can happen in a baseball game, and the better team doesn't always win. A superior team can blow out an inferior team one day and be blown out by that very team the next day. It really is a game of inches.

But in spite of the level of luck and chance, the players in this book were a cut above (or in some cases several cuts above) the average player. Also included are notable non-playing characters such as manager Paul Richards and Commissioner Kenesaw Mountain Landis. Several were choice individuals and so highly regarded that they achieved virtual sainthood. Then we have a few good men. Sadly, several fall under the "Life isn't Fair" category. Finally, some were complex and mysterious enough that we are forced to ask, as Butch Cassidy asked The Sundance Kid, "Who Are Those Guys?"

My late, dear friend, Tom Parrish, to whom *Beyond the Ballpark* was dedicated, once confronted one of his caregivers, whom he affectionately called "Bruiser," that she seemed always to be arguing with him. Bruiser replied, "I'm not arguing. I'm just *explaining* things to you." Likewise, I try to explain to the reader what made these guys tick. I hope it is an enjoyable read even if you don't always agree with my assessment of them.

Under each category, the individuals will be listed in chronological order, the key date being the beginning of their major league career.

PART I

"WHEN THE SAINTS GO MARCHING IN"

I t's pretty rare for any athlete to be called a saint. Especially in today's world where the lives of star athletes are often examined under a microscope. The slightest misstep may be blown out of proportion. Furthermore, fans are often a fickle lot. On the one hand they may set up shrines in their homes for their favorite players, and then turn on them with a vengeance if they stray too far.

This was not always the case. In earlier years sportswriters rarely, if ever, wrote about the private lives of athletes. They knew about, and often witnessed, the drinking and carousing of ball players, or the way they treated their families and fans. But they ignored those flaws in their reports. Some observers point to Jim Bouton's *Ball Four* as a major turning point in sports reporting. His tell all book opened a window into the personal lives of several of his Yankee teammates. It proved to be a bombshell. Now other writers felt free to report negative things about the stars of the day.

In my previous baseball book, *Beyond the Ballpark: The Honorable, Immoral, and Eccentric Lives of Baseball Legends*, I didn't have a category of "Saints" or "Really Good Guys," but if I had at least two of the "Good Guys" would have qualified. In my judgment Walter Johnson may have been the finest human being to ever set foot on a ball diamond. George Kell would be a close second. These two men were admired, and even loved, by teammates and foes alike. It would be hard to find a negative statement relating to their moral character.

The five players listed as saints in this book might not quite place them alongside Johnson and Kell, but they deserve a place in the moral Mt. Rushmore of baseball. Their lives were exceptional. May their tribe increase.

Harry Hooper
1887-1974
Career: 1909-1925

Harry Bartholomew Hooper was a right fielder who played for the Boston Red Sox and Chicago White Sox. He was elected to the Hall of Fame in 1971.

Good guy Harry Hooper is not exactly a household name, even within households containing baseball fanatics, even though he, along with Tris Speaker and Duffy Lewis, was a member of what many experts believe to be the greatest outfield of all time. Hooper was overshadowed during his time by such greats as Speaker, Ty Cobb, Babe Ruth, Christy Mathewson, Cy Young, and Walter Johnson. He was less a Superman than an Everyman.[2] He possessed none of the flamboyance of a Ruth or a Cobb but went about the game in a business- like

---

[2] As described by his biographer Paul Zingg, Harry Hooper: An American Baseball Life. University of Illinois Press, 2004, 4.

manner. He was a consummate professional in a day when baseball was finally shedding its rough neck image due to an influx of college educated men like himself. These men were slowly replacing the rowdy bunch who spent their off hours in bars and brothels.

Hooper's restless father left the east coast and lived briefly in numerous places before settling down to farm in California, where Harry was born. Harry was such a bright child that his family realized that education would become a major part of his life. Harry fell in love with baseball at a very early age, and he eventually attended St. Mary's College in Oakland, a private Catholic college that would send several players to the Major Leagues. Although he seems to have initially "majored in baseball," he was so proficient in math and the sciences that he became a first- rate engineer and probably would have pursued that as a profession had not opportunities opened up to enable him to play professional baseball. He approached the game like a dedicated engineer would approach a project - - - with fierce attention to detail and a pursuit of excellence. His study of the game and his dedication to a high level of physical conditioning enabled him to achieve what came easier and naturally to more gifted athletes. He might not have had the near pathological work ethic of Ty Cobb (who did?), but he wasn't far behind. He earned nothing but respect from his teammates and from his opponents. Negative statements about him are hard to find.

Like most teams at that time, the Red Sox were a cliquish and divided team. Speaker and Lewis disliked each other intensely and rarely spoke to each other. Although Hooper had his close friends on the club, most notably Smokey Joe Wood and Larry Gardner, Hooper got along well with all members of the team and seemed to function as a unifying force. No doubt this was the reason he was named captain of the team. In fact, managers Jack Barry and Ed Barrow depended heavily upon Hooper's advice in all aspects of the game. Hooper is credited with pushing Barrow to play the Babe in the field on the days he didn't pitch, recognizing that fans came to the park to see Ruth hit more than to see him pitch. Hooper tutored the Babe in the fine points of playing the outfield.

Hooper's analytical and people skills were especially on display when he virtually single-handedly averted a players' strike during the 1918 World Series between the Red Sox and the Chicago Cubs. Players on both teams were upset with the new system of how the proceeds from the Series were distributed, the brainchild of the dreaded Commissioner Ban Johnson. Hooper walked a fine line between defending the players' dissatisfaction and a realization of how damaging a strike would be to baseball. Unfortunately, Johnson later reneged on his agreement and punished the players by denying them the World Series emblems that were traditionally awarded the winners. For several years after this ugly deed Hooper sought to rectify the damage, but he was unsuccessful in persuading later Commissioners to right this wrong. Throughout this entire episode, Hooper's stock rose among the players, the management, and the press. Everyone acknowledged his integrity, his intelligence, and his commitment to fairness.

Hooper was especially sickened by the Black Sox scandal. He had harsh words for Comiskey, who was a stingy owner, and for both Hal Chase and Chick Gandil, who he saw as morally corrupt. Thus, he saw the Sox's downfall as the result of both terrible management and a few crooked players.

The affection in which he was held in Boston was seen at Hooper's first appearance at Fenway Park following his trade to the White Sox in 1921. The fans gave him a huge ovation when he came to bat for the first time, reducing Hooper to tears. Later, the Red Sox scheduled an official day of recognition of his contribution to Red Sox baseball. It also speaks volumes that although Hooper enjoyed some of his best years individually with the White Sox, he was frustrated because of the team's poor showing. Hooper proved time and again that he was the ultimate team player who always put the team above his personal goals and accomplishments.

A few years after retirement Hooper was offered the job of managing the Princeton baseball team, which he did for two years. This was largely an unsuccessful venture, although he restored some competitive respectability to the program. The best thing that came from this stint was the good fortune of having Tris Speaker assist him in developing players. These two years brought Harry and Tris much closer together and deepened their friendship. Their affection for each other was evident at Old Timers' games and at other baseball events. Speaker was insistent that Hooper belonged along-side him in the Hall of Fame. After several misses, he finally received enough votes in 1971, with a strong assist from his son, John, who campaigned hard for his father. Hooper thoroughly enjoyed his subsequent trips to Cooperstown.

Hooper left behind what few players of the olden days left us: a sizeable cache of correspondence. Most of what is preserved contains the letters to his beloved wife, Esther. Hooper comes across as the educated man he was, but also as one who adored his wife and was not hesitant to express his intense affection for her. Esther stayed in California during most of Hooper's tenure in Boston, and the long season's separation was difficult for Harry. He seemed to cope by writing lengthy letters to the most important person in his life. It is not surprising that when Esther died in 1969, Harry descended into a deep depression that never really left him during the intervening five years prior to his death. Although he went about his life with the support of his children and friends, there was an apparent sadness.

Hooper's trusting and generous nature left him vulnerable to those who sought to bring him into their various business ventures. Although they might have been well-intentioned, Hooper suffered several financial setbacks in oil drilling and insurance ventures by following bad advice from acquaintances.

Fortunately, he had a good eye for coastal property and those investments enabled him to live securely in his life after baseball.

Hooper's support for Franklin Roosevelt brought him the offer to become the postmaster of the small town of Capitola, California. The job didn't interfere with his other responsibilities and enabled him to have a steady income for twenty-four years before he retired at age seventy.

Hooper remained close to his three children and several grandchildren while also becoming involved in various civic and environmental activities, most notably the protection of the California coastal wetlands.

A stroke in 1974 severely restricted the activities of the eighty-seven-year-old Hall of Famer. Before being wheeled into surgery to treat an aneurysm, Hooper reassured his son Harry, Jr. with his last words, "Don't worry, son. I've had a good life." He died during the surgery.

Glowing testimonials in newspapers across the country and floral arrangements from all over graced his funeral service. Even JFK's mother, Rose Kennedy, sent flowers. The persistent themes describing him were his sterling character and the way he played the game with class and skill. He was a true craftsman of the game, and as his friend Larry Gardner said, "He was a class act."[3]

---

[3]   Cited in Zingg, 223.

Pepper Martin
1904-1965
Career: 1928-1944

Pepper Martin was a third baseman who spent his entire career with the St. Louis Cardinals. Although a fine ballplayer, he is included in our study mostly because he was so colorful, interesting, and beloved.

Some of the subjects of our study are complex characters who wrestled with inner demons while others are more transparent, so "what you see is what you get." Martin falls into the latter category.

John Leonard Roosevelt (after Teddy) Martin said that he was called "Pepper" by Blake Harper, who was in charge of concessions at Sportsman Park in Ft. Smith, Arkansas, because of the way Martin hopped around the base paths and because of the way he talked. Martin liked the name so much that he later had his name legally changed to Pepper. His other moniker, "The Wild Horse of the Osage," was penned by Cray Remington, a Rochester, N.Y., newspaperman, as a way of describing Martin's aggressive and daring base running.

Martin was fortunate to find a like-minded spouse when, as he says, Martin "committed matrimony" with eighteen-year-old Ruby Pope in 1927. Like Martin, Ruby loved to hunt and was a crack shot, and they spent many hours together hunting quail, rabbit, and duck. She also proved to be a healthy restraining influence on Pepper's spending habits. From all accounts they had a wonderful marriage. Although he yearned for a son, he was very close to all three of his daughters.

His boyish enthusiasm for the game endeared him to fans and teammates alike. He was the embodiment of this famous (or infamous) Cardinals team referred to as The Gashouse Gang. This ordinary looking man with a grimy Cardinals' uniform (it would be dirty after only a few minutes on the diamond) possessed a modesty that wasn't fake or contrived, and people loved him for it. He was cheered even in opposing ballparks. His headfirst belly flopping style always brought cheers from the crowd. Nobody hustled more than Pepper. One sportswriter, Bob Chieger, described Martin as "a chunky, unshaven hobo who ran bases like a berserk locomotive, slept in the raw, and swore at pitchers in his sleep."[4]

He entered celebrity status following his remarkable performance in the 1931 World Series against the powerful Philadelphia A's. Even though the A's had superstars like Foxx, Simmons, and Grove, and the Cards had future Hall of Famers like Frisch, Bottomley, and Hafey, Martin stole the show that year. Even though the game had become mostly slugging contests, Martin was a throwback to the Cobb era, where speed and trickery decided games and his style certainly determined the outcome of this World Series. Surprisingly, he became a national celebrity, the Babe Ruth of the National League, and was even voted Athlete of the Year by the Associated Press.

Pepper's celebrity status meant that he would be pursued by the press, and he always seemed to come up with a humorous quote. Regarding his new-found status he remarked, "Ain't that all the bunk. If I strike out tomorrow with a couple of men on base, they will give me the razberry. But it is nice to hear it

---

[4]   Cited in John Heidenry, *The Gashouse Gang*. Public Affairs, 2007, 95.

once in a while - makes you feel good."[5] He remarked to one reporter that "A few months ago no one cared whether I could write my own name. Now I have signed it on everything from a paper towel to a postage stamp."[6]

Pepper's new-found popularity didn't go to his head. Following the Series Martin said in an interview that "I know there was a lot of luck in what I did, and I want everybody to know that Pepper Martin will always be as common as Oklahoma dirt. Nobody need think that I'll get the swell head just because I was lucky to get hits off Grove and Earnshaw and steal a few bases. . . I'm not promising to be a star or anything like that, but I'm going to bear down and do my best."[7]

In 1939 the Cardinals brought in a new manager who was big on discipline and demanded a lot of physical, hard work. In his usual fashion Martin quipped, "I got a jackass back in Oklahoma, and you can work him from sunup till sundown and he ain't never gonna win the Kentucky Derby."[8]

Following his playing career Pepper managed for a time in the Florida International League. On one occasion when an umpire's call didn't go his team's way, he remarked to a reporter that "I looked at my two hands and darned if I didn't have an umpire's throat between them."[9]

In 1959 the Gas House Gang was reassembled to celebrate the 25th anniversary of the 1934 championship. At this event owner Branch Rickey commented that Martin was a fellow who would kill you in a game and then sit up all night with you to get well. The notorious penny-pinching Rickey also noted that the team loved the game so much that "by Judas Priest I believe

---

[5] Cited in Thomas Barthel, *Pepper Martin: A Baseball Biography.* McFarland a & Co., 2003, 87. Much of the information about Martin in this essay is culled from this book.

[6] *Ibid.*, 91.

[7] *Ibid.*, 99.

[8] Cited in Barthel, 151.

[9] *Ibid.*, 191.

these boys would have played for nothing." Pepper responded in a loud whisper, "By John Brown, Mr. Rickey, we almost did."[10] Years before Rickey said that Pepper was the most genuine person he had ever met in his life and that there was never an ounce of pretense in the man.[11]

While on the subject of the Gas House Gang, we should compare Martin with the incomparable Dizzy Dean. Pepper was six years older than Dizzy, acted like Dean's older brother, and tried to guide the irrepressible Dean to be more responsible. Pepper's famous pranks were planned beforehand, carefully selected, and didn't offend people, whereas Dean's loudmouth and pranks at times caused trouble. The two remained close, however, with Dean often staying in the Martin home, where he delighted in playing with Martin's daughters. They also liked to wrestle in the clubhouse, sometimes to the point of injuring themselves.

Besides the fairly common pranks like the hot foot, the sneezing powder placed in a newspaper, the water balloon drops out of the hotel windows, and tying the manager's uniform in knots, Martin is best remembered for barging into a Rotary banquet in a hotel ballroom with Dizzy and another teammate disguised as maintenance men, where they proceeded to hammer on the ceiling and talk loudly about what color to paint the room while also bumping into tables and moving chairs around, usually with people still in them. After the hotel manager was summoned, the identity of the men was uncovered to the great delight of the audience who cheered them, invited them to the head table, and even asked them to give talks.[12] At another hotel he was asked to leave after he was found shooting at pigeons from his hotel window. Martin's pranks might be annoying and startling, but they were never mean.

---

[10] *Ibid.*, 211.
[11] Cited in Heidenry, 121.
[12] See the full account in Barthel, 130.

Martin's pranks kept the team loose during a long season and didn't allow anyone to become too self-important. His antics, no doubt, brought many gray hairs to manager Frankie Frisch.

One example of his brand of mischief occurred when the Cardinals were playing the Giants, with Ole Diz pitching. Bill Terry's first at bat was a screamer that hit Diz on the shin. Terry's second at bat saw the ball hit so hard that it knocked Diz's glove off his hand. When Terry came up for his third at bat, Pepper ambled over to the mound and asked Dean if he would accept some advice. Sure, said Dean. Pepper said, "I don't think you're playing deep enough."[13]

Martin impressed people with his honesty and integrity, but he also had a pugnacious streak and engaged in fights on occasion. Biographer Thomas Barthel nicely sums up Pepper's personality: "Martin was an interesting mix of honest man, cheat, fierce competitor, courtly gentleman, and prankster. No one seemed to know which one he was about to be next."[14] Hall of Fame Umpire Bill Klem believed that Martin was "as authentic as a 60-second minute. His whim, impulses and mad inspirations stemmed from an honest, prankish fun-loving soul. . . of a grown-up man who still thought a boy's life was pretty swell. . ."[15]

Martin shied away from alcohol, apparently because of what alcoholism had done to his brother Charlie. As a manager he responded harshly to players whose drinking affected the play of the team.

Martin's wife Ruby was a very religious woman who was active in a Baptist church. Earlier Pepper was described by his daughter as being "quietly religious," but due to Ruby's influence Martin became more religious as he aged, was seen

---

[13] Cited in Peter Williams, *When the Giants Were Giants: Bill Terry and the Golden Age of New York Baseball.* Algonquin Books of Chapel Hill, 1994, 185.

[14] Barthel, 140.

[15] Cited in Barthel, 154.

reading the Bible in the dugout, and even taught a Sunday School class. He contributed enough to the life of the Blocker (Oklahoma) Baptist Church that an addition to the sanctuary was named "The Pepper Martin Memorial Auditorium." His faith brought him a conspicuous measure of serenity in his later years. His delightful sense of humor and his genuine love of people made him a popular speaker. He never "spoke and ran" but enjoyed meeting everybody in the room.

Martin died of a heart attack at the relatively young age of 61. Four hundred people attended the funeral service at the First Baptist Church of McAlester, Oklahoma, where they heard it said that "Pepper Martin is safe at home. He did not have to steal home as he did so many times."[16] Honorary pallbearers included baseball men Allie Reynolds, Mickey Owen, and Branch Rickey.

It was said that he still had the body of a twenty-year old. If our current knowledge of cardiology had existed at his time, he would have had open heart surgery or a stent and probably lived many more years. And those years would have brought laughs and happiness to many people.

---

[16]   Barthel, 218.

Stan Musial
1920-2013
Playing Career: 1941-63
Nickname: "Stan the Man"

Stanley Frank Musial was an outfielder/infielder for the St. Louis Cardinals. He was elected to the Hall of Fame in 1969.

Stan's father, Lukasz Musial, of Polish descent, was born in then Austria-Hungary. His mother, Mary Lancos, was of Czech descent and born in New York City. They settled in Donora, Pennsylvania, where Lukasz worked in the steel mill. Stan was close to his mother but had a more strained relationship with his father, who struggled with alcohol. His father's problems with alcohol, however, didn't propel Stan towards abstinence. He was a social drinker throughout his adult life. The family regularly attended St. Michael's Orthodox Catholic Church.

In school, Stan was an average student at best and always

the best athlete in every school he attended. He was shy and developed a stammer he carried into adulthood.[17]

As a teen, Stan worked at a grocery store owned by Sam Labash, a former baseball player. Sam had found just the kind of guy for his daughter Lillian. Stan claimed that he and Lillian were secretly married on Stan's birthday, November 21, 1939, but a church wedding was held on May 25, 1940, in Daytona Beach, Florida, where Stan had gone for spring training. Their first child was born in August of that year. Although baseball and business interests took Stan away from home a great deal, the marriage and family life appeared to be strong.

Interestingly, Stan came by his famous moniker not in St. Louis, but in Brooklyn. Dodger fans took to Stan, and every time he came to the plate they would chant "Here comes the man!" After a sportswriter wrote about it, this became his nickname for life. It was not uncommon for Dodger fans to give him a standing ovation. Dodger fans had earlier adopted Dixie Walker ("The People's Choice") and Gil Hodges (never booed) as their favorite Dodgers; now they adopted Stan as their favorite opponent. Interesting fans, those Dodger rooters.[18]

One will search in vain to find a more beloved figure in St. Louis than Stan Musial. Stan endeared himself to everyone

---

[17] Musial's biographer, George Vecsey, notes that Stan, a left-hander, was forced to write right-handed in school. Vecsey cites a major study in 1933 linking stuttering to the forcing of a left-hander to write right-handed which changed patterns in the brain. George Vecsey, *Stan Musial: An American Life*. Ballantine Books, 2011, 40f.

[18] One Dodger rooter compared Dodger fans to Yankee fans, saying Yankee fans had an essential meanness because they felt like God owed them championships whereas Dodger fans were so often beaten down that they had an essential humility and understanding not possible for Yankee fans. Dodger fans also learned that there was more to the games than just winning. They learned to care about excellence, even if it's someone else's excellence. Musial often got standing ovations at Ebbets Field. Cited in Peter Golenbock's *Bums: An Oral History of the Brooklyn Dodgers*. Contemporary Books, 2000, 442f.

who met him. He was accessible to any and all. He answered the phone from fans and his house seemed to always have kids hanging around it. Until his health failed him in his 90s, he would attend Cardinals games, linger at his statue there and entertain fans with his harmonica playing.

Even opposing players had nothing but praise for the affable Musial. Robin Roberts, who pitched against Musial many times, said Stan always seemed to be in a good mood and went out of his way to complement Roberts when he made a good play. Roberts remembers an instance when a big fight broke out between the Cardinals and the Phillies. Musial grabbed his arm and said, "Robin, we're making too much money to get hurt in something like this." Roberts quickly agreed.[19]

Following a disastrous outing in the 1960 All-Star game, Boston Red Sox pitcher Bill Monbouquette expressed great admiration for Musial when Stan insisted that Monbouquette, sitting in the hotel lobby brooding after the game, accompany a group of players to dinner. Stan even picked up the tab for everybody.[20] One could cite many similar instances of Musial's spontaneous generosity. One time roommate Hank Sauer observed that "If you couldn't get along with Musial, you couldn't get along with anybody. . .He was a superstar and a super person."[21] Teammate Tim McCarver gushed that Stan was a "man who can captivate a room without even anyone knowing that he's there. You could feel him in a room and a lot of great men I hear are like that. But with Musial it was very, very special."[22]

Stan's reaction to Jackie Robinson's arrival in the major leagues revealed elements of his character. Musial, in keeping

---

[19] Robin Roberts with C. Paul Rogers III, *My Life in Baseball*. Triumph Books, 2003, 43f, 77.

[20] Danny Peary (Ed.), *We Played the Game: Memories of Baseball's Greatest Era*. Black Dog & Leventhal, 1994, 485.

[21] *Ibid.*, 322.

[22] Cited in Vecsey, 15.

with his life-long discomfort with conflict, stayed above the fray, leading Jackie to say that Musial was a nice guy, but when it came to Jackie breaking the color barrier, Musial neither hurt nor helped him. Jackie wished that Stan had not been so passive.[23] On the other hand Willie Mays had high praise for Musial not only as a ball player, but because Musial insisted on joining a card game with all black players while on an airplane headed to an All-Star game. Mays added, "That told me how classy he was, and I never forgot that."[24]

Although there are several versions of the interactions between players in the infamous spiking incident when the rough-and-tumble Enos Slaughter spiked Jackie at first base, all versions show Stan as understanding the frustrations Jackie faced and empathizing with Jackie's desire for revenge. One version even has Stan and Slaughter fighting over the incident.[25]

Another racial issue connected with Musial was the matter of Curt Flood's challenge of the reserve clause. Flood viewed Stan as a great guy but "unfathomably naïve," who, because he was an authentic superstar, was remote from the difficulties encountered by lesser athletes. As general manager of the Cardinals after his playing days, Musial understandably embraced management's point of view concerning conflicts with players. Flood viewed Musial as believing that the current arrangement was best for everybody connected with baseball. "(Musial) saw the world entirely in terms of his own good fortune."[26]

In his book examining the issues surrounding Flood's challenging of the baseball establishment, Baseball writer Brad Snyder notes that Musial was deeply hurt by the comments Flood

---

[23] Vecsey 163.
[24] James S. Hirsch, *Willie Mays: The Life, the Legend.* Scribner, 2010, 230f.
[25] Vecsey, 160f. See the angry reactions to this incident by Dodger players Rex Barney, Ralph Branca and Carl Furillo in Gollenbock, 156f.
[26] Cited in *Ibid.,* 245f.

made about him in his autobiography. Flood also complains that he and his date were denied service in Stan and Biggie's restaurant late one evening, but Musial said the restaurant would have denied anyone service because it was closing time. Flood's description of Stan as "a simpleminded company man" and his derision of Stan's regular use of "wunnerful" added to Stan's anguish, and certainly further alienated Cardinals fans who might otherwise have been more sympathetic to Flood.[27]

But a revealing incident which shows Musial standing up for minorities occurred in a cab ride with an unnamed teammate. The player noticed a Jewish name on the cabbie's placard and started speaking in a crude version of a Jewish accent. Stan told him to cease and desist. When they arrived at the ballpark the teammate tried to pay for the ride, but Musial insisted on paying, and then warned the teammate to never get in a cab with him.[28]

Whereas most ballplayers then (and now) steer clear of politics, Musial was an active and life-long Democrat. He campaigned on behalf of John Kennedy and later visited with him often in the Oval Office. Stan told his close friend, author James Michener, that he supported Kennedy because of JFK's talk about a more just society: "All that I have I got because older men helped me. That why I'm for Kennedy."[29]

In retirement, Musial stayed busy on many fronts. He was a regular greeter at his popular restaurant, co-owned with Biggie Garagnani ("Stan's and Biggie's"). He was often in the Cardinals 'press box. He and Lil enjoyed traveling.

An unfortunate chapter in Stan's life centered around his relationship with Joe Garagiola. The two met in 1941 and became very close friends and eventually became business partners in 1958, co-owning a bowling alley. When a news

---

27 Brad Snyder, *A Well-Paid Slave: Curt Flood's Fight for Free Agency in Professional Sports.* Viking, 2006, 211.

28 Cited in Vecsey, 215.

29 *Ibid.,* 235.

headline in 1986 read that Joe had filed a suit against Musial and his sons, the city of St. Louis was stunned. The suit was eventually settled out of court, with both sides pledging confidentiality. The rift between Stan and Joe was permanent. Both said negative things about the other, with Garagiola going so far as to say that he had come to realize that Musial was not a nice person. The rift made for tense situations as both were still involved in Cardinals and city activities. It is telling that the only Hall of Fame induction ceremony that Musial didn't attend was the year Garagiola was inducted in the broadcaster's wing of the Hall. Biographer Vecsey concludes that this "ruined friendship hung over Musial, exposed a melancholy side, a trace of vindictiveness. Or maybe it was old age coming on."[30] A person close to Musial noted that Stan wasn't a lot of fun for a year or so after the split.

A great honor was bestowed on Musial when he received the Presidential Medal of Freedom in 2011, an award given previously to both DiMaggio and Williams. President Obama reminded the guests that there was so much more to the man than his remarkable playing career. "Stan remains to this day, an icon, untarnished, a beloved pillar of the community; a gentleman you'd want your kids to emulate."[31]

Surgery for prostate cancer slowed down Musial for a year or so, but he was back doing his thing afterwards. A much more serious problem began to develop in his mid-eighties when he was diagnosed with Alzheimer's disease. The family pitched in to help keep him active as possible, but the slow descent was inevitable.

Musial died in his home at age 92. He had earlier requested that high profile announcer Bob Costas speak at his funeral, and the family honored his wishes. Hundreds filled the Cathedral Basilica in St. Louis, including Hall of Famers Bob Gibson, Lou

---

30   *Ibid.*, 319f.
31   Cited in Vecsey, 335.

Brock, Ozzie Smith, Bruce Sutter, Joe Torre, and 90-year-old former roommate Red Schoendienst while thousands stood outside in the January cold to honor their beloved hero. The two-hour Mass was highlighted by Costas' emotional and moving eulogy where Costas said that Musial's achievement was "more than two decades of sustained excellence as a baseball player and more than nine decades as a thoroughly decent human being."[32] He was buried in Bellerive Heritage Gardens in the St. Louis suburb of Creve Coeur next to his wife Lil, who had died a year earlier.

---

[32] "Cardinal legend Stan Musial remembered at funeral Mass." Associated Press, January 26, 2013. Costas' entire nineteen-minute eulogy is available on YouTube. Costas also noted that Musial, though ill, flew down to Mickey Mantle's funeral in Dallas and stood against the wall at the back of the church throughout the ceremony. It probably didn't enter Stan's mind that he could demand special treatment and seating arrangements.

Gil Hodges
1924-1972
Career: Player: 1943-1963; Mgr.: 1962-1971

Gil Hodges was a first baseman for the Brooklyn Dodgers, and later manager of the New York Mets. He was (surely many of his fans said: "finally!!") voted into the Hall of Fame in 2021

Gil Hodges ranks up there with Walter Johnson and George Kell when it comes to character and decency. It's virtually impossible to find anybody who ever said anything negative about this gentle giant. Like Johnson and Pepper Martin, "St. Gilbert" died much too young. One always hopes that people who bring such delight to others could enjoy a long and prosperous life. Sportswriters Rob Neyer and Eddie Epstein remind us that "Few things elicit more sentiment than a good or great baseball player who left the earth a little early...There's no better way to make a fifty-year old baseball fan teary-eyed than to start talking about the erstwhile Dodger first baseman."[33]

---

[33] Rob Neyer and Eddie Epstein, *Baseball Dynasties: The Greatest Teams of All Time*. W.W. Norton, 200, 211.

Yogi Berra's biographer, Allen Barra, wrote that "If a poll had been taken in 1968 among players, managers, and front office people, Gil Hodges would probably have been named as the most respected man in baseball. A near Hall of Fame first baseman, he was smart, authoritative, and the natural leader that many managers pretend to be."[34] It is not surprising that Hodges was the only player never booed at Ebbets Field. Unfortunately, Gil seemed to have inherited a genetic tendency toward heart disease (his father and brother died of massive heart attacks) and, combined with heavy smoking and the stress of the game proved too much for this much loved and admired man.

Although Hodges was only recently voted into the Hall-of-Famer, for years all of his teammates insisted that he belonged there, and a few knowledgeable experts agreed.[35] Be that as it may, Hodges belongs in this book because of his contribution to the game and because of his character and personality.

Gil was the son of a small-town coal miner in southern Indiana but inherited his mother's wonderful disposition. Being raised in a small town where everyone knew each other affords biographers a good opportunity to interview many people who knew their subject and his families. In order to talk to as many people as possible who had experienced extensive contact with Hodges during Gil's youth and Gil's subsequent visits to his hometown, in the late 1980s biographer and Dodgers fan Marino Amoruso [36] took the trek to Petersburg, Indiana. The

[34] Allen Barra, *Yogi Berra: Eternal Yankee*. W.W. Norton, 2009, 323.

[35] The guru of baseball statistics, Bill James, ranks Hodges as only the 30th best first baseman behind a large number of first baseman not in the Hall of Fame. James acknowledges that Hodges may have made it into the Hall had he played his entire career at shortstop, his original position. James also acknowledges that Hodges was indeed a beloved player and deservingly so. Bill James, *The New Bill James Historical Baseball Abstract*. Free Press, 2001, 443.

[36] Marino Amoruso, *Gil Hodges: The Quiet Man*. Paul S. Erikksson, 1991.

townspeople's assessment of Gil matched what Amoruso found among his teammates: nothing but praise and admiration.

Hodges impressed all who knew him with his devotion to his family. His wife Joan and his children occupied first place on his list of priorities.[37] Joan bragged to one writer how much help Gil was around the house and with the children. It echoes one writer's assessment: "We think of Willie Mays as a great ballplayer who also happens to be married. We think of Gil Hodges as a warm and loving family man, who happens to play ball for a living."[38] His children viewed him as a very strict father, yet lovingly devoted to them. Gil Jr. remembers that his father taught them that, "The one thing that you don't do in life is lie." [39]

There is not the slightest hint of any womanizing, which is, as we have noted throughout our study, a fairly common trait among ballplayers of every era. Ballplayers on the road are veritably swamped with opportunities to engage in sex with as many women as their appetites demand. Gil was not a part of that lifestyle. He seemed motivated not out of a sense of duty, although his deeply held Roman Catholic convictions help imbue a sense of duty, but more because he genuinely enjoyed being with his family. Brooklyn residents were usually surprised to see Gil helping with the grocery shopping when many other players tried to avoid being in public, or apparently felt that grocery shopping was beneath them.

---

[37] As of this writing Gil's wife, Joan, born in 1926, still lives in the same house in the Flatbush section of Brooklyn that they shared during his baseball days. One son, Gil, Jr., who runs a private investigation business in the New York area, noted that even though his father is not in the Hall of Fame, it is irrelevant because "everybody treats him like his is in the Hall." Cited in Dave George, "Commentary: Recalling Gil Hodges, the dearly missed Dodger who died 40 years ago Monday." *Palm Beach Post*, March 31, 2012.

[38] Tom Clavin and Danny Peary, *Gil Hodges: The Brooklyn Bums, The Miracle Mets, and the Extraordinary Life of a Baseball Legend.* New American Library, 2013, 249.

[39] *Ibid.*, 281.

Hodges didn't wear his patriotism on his sleeve, but he was proud of his service in the Marines, and always stood at strict attention during the playing of the national anthem prior to ball games. Interestingly, he participated in the battles on Iwo Jima and Okinowa, but like many returning veterans of his generation, never talked with anyone about his experiences there. Knowing what we know about the horrors of those weeks of incredible death and bloodshed, one wonders what might have been buried deep within Gil's psyche that he found incapable of sharing with even his close friends. But his reticence in this matter matches his general tendency of keeping his feelings and emotions private.

One might know what Gil was thinking, but usually couldn't know what was happening in his gut. Even his good friend and teammate Pee Wee Reese wondered if Gil's keeping everything inside might have contributed to his heart attacks. Reese also saw Hodges as a stabilizing influence in the clubhouse, especially when emotions were running high. Another teammate, Duke Snider, shared this perspective: "Gil was one of a kind, a quiet ex-Marine who kept his feelings and emotions inside, but as a tower of strength for the whole team. . .Through his years as a Dodger, Gil remained a quiet leader, never showing his emotions. One day, though, I got a glimpse of those emotions. Gil smoked a lot. It wasn't unusual for him to sneak a cigarette on the bench even though it's against major-league rules. I saw him this particular day light up on the bench during a close game, and his hands were shaking so much he could hardly light the cigarette. After that I watched him every time he would light up, and it was always the same. His hands were shaking. That told me there was a lot more going on inside Gil than he was willing to show." [40]

Gil's calm demeanor helped to diffuse explosive situations,

---

[40] Duke Snider with Bill Gilbert, *The Duke of Flatbush*. Zebra Books, 1988, 70f.

and he was often the one in the middle of a fight trying to break it up.[41] Those who played for him could recall only a few rare instances when Gil lost his cool and let his true feelings explode. He was quiet on the outside, but apparently not so quiet on the inside. With a stoic, one never really knows what is happening within. Amuruso is probably on target when he observes, "It is ironic that many of the qualities for which Hodges was admired and loved were also personality characteristics that in some measure contributed to his early heart disease." [42] It is common medical knowledge that keeping emotions bottled-up can-do damage to internal organs like the heart. When it comes to expressing emotions, some people are turtles, and some are skunks. Gil was clearly a turtle.

Teammate Carl Erskine also noted the irony of seeing the two strongest men on the field, Hodges and Jackie Robinson, developing health problems that led them to premature deaths.

As a manager, he was more like Joe McCarthy, Connie Mack, and Al Lopez, and not like the fiery John McGraw and Leo Durocher. Hodges never criticized a player in front of others, but drew the offender aside and used the incident as a teaching moment. He saw no benefit in embarrassing or shaming a player. To him, that would be treating a player disrespectfully. And all who knew him unanimously concluded that Gil treated everyone he encountered with respect. He did so by both treating everybody alike while handling them differently. He studied the game thoroughly but seemed instinctively to know how to motivate a player.

Although Hodges rarely spoke about his religious convictions, he was a devout Catholic. He was regular in attendance at Mass, and he certainly embodied what many would describe as "a good Catholic." Father Charles Curley, Gil's friend and

---

[41] One such humorous incident occurred in a Dodger game against the Braves where Hodges grabbed the foot of the pugnacious and powerfully built Eddie Mathews and drug him to the Braves dugout and asked, "where shall I deposit him?" Amoruso, 33.

[42] *Ibid.*, 26.

pastor of Our Lady Help of Christians near Hodges' home in Brooklyn, said at Gil's funeral service that Gil was "a hero of authentic stamp," and "an ornament to his parish." [43]

One catches a glimpse of a person's character when they are "off screen" or dealing with a "nobody." One such moment occurred when Gil returned to his hometown for his grandmother's funeral. Once, he was introduced to a crippled young girl, who, when told that she was meeting a celebrity who played ball on television, responded, "So what?" Gil just chuckled and was later seen with the young girl sitting on his lap and asking Gil to accompany her to school the next day. Gil said he would love to but had to return immediately to rejoin his team. [44] It is not common for high profile people to show such interest and respect to those who have nothing to offer them. It shows a lot about Gil's character. He strongly believed that ball players had the responsibility to be good role models for young people. A player fulfilled this responsibility through both words and conduct. No one could accuse him of not practicing what he preached.

Sportswriter Joseph Durso describes Hodges as "reverent, friendly, strong and silent. He had a reputation of shooting straight, and he kept his hands in his back pockets when arguing with umpires. He was a kind of middle-aged Eagle Scout." [45]

His teammates spoke of him in the same way. Minor league teammate Bill Hardy said that Hodges was a "soft-spoken, giant gentleman who never said a harsh word to or about anybody. I can't say how much I respected him." His rookie year roommate Ralph Branca described Hodges as "a regular, likeable guy. He was basically quiet, but if you got him to talk you'd discover that he had a great sense of humor, a dry wit, and, if you to

---

[43] Cited in Red Smith, "Gil and His Guys Last Time Around, *New York Times*, April 7, 1972, 17.

[44] Amoruso, 185.

[45] Joseph Durso, Transformer of Mets," *New York Times*, April 3, 1972, 52. Hodges was never thrown out of a game during his entire career.

know him, he'd bust you a little." Ed Roebuck said he was a role model for everybody. Roy Campanella said that Gil was "the greatest guy I ever had the pleasure to play with." In his rookie year Don Drysdale was assigned to room with Hodges and said it felt like rooming with a saint. "All you had to do was watch how he carried himself, on and off the field, and you knew that his was the right way of going about being a major league ballplayer."[46]

Hodges displayed an innate ability to read people and to discover what made them tick. He impressed those he managed with his insights into players as well as his keen baseball knowledge. He knew how to instill confidence in a player who was having a tough time, and he knew when it was best to say nothing at all.

To those on the outside, Hodges appeared to be a dead serious guy; but he also had a humorous side to him, enough of a deadpan comic that he could occasionally pull a joke on his teammates. Teammate Pee Wee Reese relates an incident in the clubhouse when he was being treated for a spike wound received while covering second base. Hodges came by and, in dead seriousness, said, "Dear me. Haven't you learned how to make that play without being spiked. It's an interesting weakness. How do you account for it, poor reflexes or lack of intelligence?" Reese, falling for the gag, yelled back, "If you're so smart, why don't you show me how to do it. You used to think you were a shortstop." "I would if I could," responded Gil, "because you honestly need help. Now that I think back on it, I realize I made that play on pure instinct and never did study the mechanics of it completely. Even as a kid I could do it perfectly. And you still have trouble with it, eh?" By now Reese knew he had been had and could only howl, "Go soak your head!" [47]

---

[46] Clavin & Peary, 61, 66, 176, 367, 194.

[47] Cited in Arthur Daley, "More Memories of Gil Hodges, *New York Times*, April 6, 1972, 57.

Mets player Donn Clendenon heaps praise on Hodges by noting that at the 1969 Mets championship reunions, it was amazing that so many of the conversations were centered around what Hodges meant to the players. Clendenon goes so far as to say that Hodges was the greatest man he ever knew.[48] Even the few players who had issues with Hodges, usually centered around not having enough playing time, came to see that Hodges was right. Ed Cranepool confesses that he was totally in the wrong when he criticized Hodges and that, in fact, Hodges made him a better player and a better person.[49]

Although Hodges suffered a heart attack at age 44, it was still a shock to all when he suffered a fatal attack just two days shy of his 48th birthday during spring training in Florida in 1972. Before boarding the plane for Florida, his wife told him to "Watch the cigarettes." Those were the last words he heard from her.[50] He apparently was the picture of health at the time and had just completed a long golf game with friends. The genes, the three pack-a-day habit, and the stress hidden within caught up much too soon with this great guy.

His baseball colleagues responded with shock. Bob Aspromonte said that Gil's death was one of the lowest points of his life. Drysdale said he was shattered and confined himself to his apartment for three days, unable to bring himself to attend the funeral or call Gil's wife. Tom Seaver brought some of Gil's things to Joan and just broke down and wept and wept.

Hodges lay in state in Our Lady of Help Roman Catholic Church in Brooklyn and 36,000 paid their respects. The next day the Mets team and many of Hodges' Dodger teammates attended the private service. Thousands lined the streets as he was taken to Holy Cross Cemetery not far from where Ebbets Field had once stood. A frail and visibly shaken Jackie

---

[48] Amoruso 107.
[49] *Ibid.*, 66.
[50] Cited in Barra, 329.

Robinson told sportswriter Roger Kahn, "Gil was always a calming presence. I always thought I'd be the first to go."[51] Only a few months later, Jackie would join Gil in the field of dreams.

The esteem in which he is held even today is seen in the fact that in Brooklyn a public school, a street, and a bridge are named in his honor. And in his hometown of Petersburg, Indiana, a bridge and a nearby monument honor the town's most famous native.

---

[51] Arnold Rampersad, *Jackie Robinson: A Biography.* Alfred A. Knopf, 1997, 455. Hodges probably did the most of any of the Dodgers to make Jackie and Rachel Robinson feel at home when Jackie joined the team. Robinson, however, was not pleased that Hodges didn't support him when Jackie became outspoken about racial issues. Sportswriter Roger Kahn quoted Jackie as saying that Stan Musial was "like Gil Hodges. A nice guy, but when it came to do what I had to do, neither one hurt me and neither one helped." Cited in George Vecsey, *Stan Musial: An American Life* . Ballantine Books, 2011, 163.

Yogi Berra
1925-2015
Playing Career: 1946-1965
Managerial Career: 1964-1985

Lawrence Peter "Yogi" Berra was a catcher for the New York Yankees. He also managed the Yankees and the New York Mets. He was elected to the Hall of Fame in 1972. Some experts believe he is the greatest catcher to play the game.

One can make the case that Yogi Berra is the most beloved athlete in American history. Even Yankee haters loved Yogi. His homespun "philosophical" observations and malapropisms spread so far beyond the baseball world that Yogi became a household word.

Born in the still mostly Italian section of St. Louis ("Dago Hill"), Yogi and his neighbor Joe Garagiola spent every free moment playing baseball. Yogi also excelled in other sports and became a schoolyard legend before rising to stardom as a Yankee.

Like many other boys of his time, Yogi left school after the

8th grade to go to work. Though uneducated, Yogi possessed a keen mind. He made smart business decisions throughout his life that brought him financial security. Furthermore, his manager, "Old Perfessor" Casey Stengel, said that Yogi "might not be a Phi Beta Kappa, but he never made a mistake on a baseball field." Stengel added, "they say he reads comic books; he plays like a goddamn genius for me."[52]

At home Berra was called "Larry," which his mother pronounced as "Lawdie." Although there have been several explanations as how he came to be called "Yogi," in his autobiography Yogi points to a time when he was thirteen or fourteen. He and his buddies went to a movie. Before the feature a short travelogue about India was shown. The boys were impressed with a man identified as a Hindu fakir and a yogi - one who practiced yoga. After leaving the movie Yogi's friend Jack Maquire, Jr. said, "You know, you look just like a yogi. I'm going to call you Yogi." Later, Yogi added a new wrinkle that went back to his American Legion playing days. In the absence of dugouts, Yogi sat on the ground with his legs crossed, looking like a yogi. Apparently the calmness and concentration exhibited by Berra confirmed his nickname even though his teammates hadn't seen the travelogue. Almost overnight, Larry became Yogi.[53] It was a perfect fit. Yogi was always even-tempered, even in the most stressful situations. In his early playing days he, like other Italians, were picked on and taunted, but Yogi just laughed it off.

Yogi regularly reacted to players and fans who kidded and taunted him about his looks. He usually would remark that he never saw anybody hit a baseball with their face. Conversely, one group of artists said that he had one of the most stimulating

---

[52]   David Cataneo, *Casey Stengel: Baseball's "Old Professor."* Cumberland House, 2003, 50f.

[53]   See the definitive biography by Allen Barra, *Yogi Berra: Eternal Yankee.* W.W. Norton & Co., 2009, 17. After he was married, however, his wife Carmen always called him Larry.

31

faces in America, adding "Yogi has the most down-to-earth face in America. It stimulates women's subconscious yearning for the Neanderthal man."[54] It is not known how Yogi responded to such glowing praise.

Not generally known is the fact that Yogi was right in the middle of the Omaha Beach invasion when he was eighteen years old. For whatever reason, Yogi seldom spoke about his war experiences. While coaching for the Houston Astros, a *Los Angeles Times* writer overheard Yogi talking about the invasion with Jim Palmer and Tim McCarver, and wrote, "Yogi survived D-Day and George Steinbrenner, and all in 40 years."[55]

Yogi's most important "homerun" was his good fortune to meet a waitress, Carmen Short, a non-Italian beauty, who admired Yogi's honesty, simplicity, and his psychological strength. Their marriage was as solid and happy as one could hope for. Letters from Yogi to Carmen while he was away playing baseball have been made public and display Yogi's deep love for his wife. After they married, Carmen converted to Catholicism, stating she "didn't have any religion on my own. I became a Catholic because it seemed to me that a religion that had such a grip on Yogi must be a good one."[56] Yogi also proved to be an engaged and attentive father to their three sons. (Trivia: one of the babysitters employed by the Berras was Martha Kostyra, the future Martha Stewart).

Yogi's interaction with Yankee General Manager George Weiss reveals Yogi's toughness and shrewdness. Weiss was considered the toughest negotiator in the game and was universally disliked, even hated, by most who knew him. Baseball historian Bert Sugar couldn't resist taking a short at Weisss, saying that only the midget Eddie Gaedel's strike zone was smaller than George Weiss's heart.[57] Yankee relief

---

54 Cited in Barra, 140.
55 Cited in Barra, 39.
56 *Ibid.*, 90.
57 Cited in Barra, 150.

ace Ryan Duren said that Weiss "was a cheap, aloof buffoon who we all hated for exploiting us."[58] Yogi insisted that he didn't dislike Weiss but noted that "he wasn't a bad guy to get to know when he wasn't working, but he was always working."[59] Yogi's first encounter with Weiss alerted him as to how the man dealt with players. Weiss offered Yogi a $500 signing bonus but Yogi found out later that he would receive the bonus only if he made the team, and that he wouldn't get it until the end of the season.[60] For several years Berra returned unsigned contracts and had to threaten retirement before the Yankees finally realized his value and pretty much let him dictate his salary.

Several well-publicized incidences reveal dimensions of Yogi's character. He had somewhat of a temper, and it was displayed in the famous "harmonica incident" involving Phil Linz, when Yogi was managing the Yankees in 1964. The Yankees had lost a doubleheader in Chicago, were on a five game losing streak, and were en route to O'Hare Airport when Linz started playing "Mary Had A Little Lamb" on his harmonica. Yogi, still stewing about his team's play, yelled back to Linz to knock it off. Apparently Linz didn't hear what Yogi said and turned to Mantle who told Linz to play it louder (or faster, as accounts differ). When Linz continued to play, Yogi walked back and told Linz to shove the harmonica up his ass. Linz replied, "You do it." Yogi slapped the harmonica out of Linz's hand, it landed on Joe Pepitone's knee who then let out a yelp of mock pain. Everyone but Yogi laughed. Author Allen Barra, noting that while Linz was being a brat and undermining his manager's authority, the real culprits of this story were Mantle and Ford, who should have

---

[58] Cited in Tom Clavin and Danny Peary, *Roger Maris: Baseball's Reluctant Hero.* Simon & Schuster, 2010, 118. Duren once received a contract on Christmas Eve offering a 25% *cut* after a year when Duren's era was 1.88.

[59] *Ibid.*, 130.

[60] Barra, 23, 27.

shown maturity and leadership in supporting their friend and manager. Yogi's job was on the line and he had a legitimate reason for being upset.[61]

Another well-known incident occurred in 1985, when Yankee owner George Steinbrenner abruptly fired Yogi only sixteen games into the season. Steinbrenner, who had earlier stated that Yogi would manage the team the entire season no matter what, publically announced Yogi's firing without even talking to Yogi. Yogi was deeply hurt and disappointed, but most of all felt disrespected and viewed such treatment as unforgivable. Yogi admitted later that the event triggered an anger in him that he didn't know existed. He vowed never to return to Yankee Stadium as long as Steinbrenner was in charge. Steinbrenner, realizing his mistake in how he handled the firing, and with special encouragement from Joe DiMaggio, beginning in 1993 sought to mend the fences. Yogi was inclined to refuse the offer, but his son Dale convinced Yogi that it would be an honorable thing to do. When Steinbrenner came to the newly founded Yogi Berra Museum in Montclair, N.J., in 1999, he apologized to Yogi, admitting that it was the worst mistake he ever made in baseball. Later that year the Yankees held a Yogi Berra Day at Yankee Stadium, when Yogi made a triumphant return to the "the House that Yogi built." Yogi announced that the feud was over, that everything was great between the two men, but couldn't resist saying that it was nice that he didn't have to work for The Boss anymore.[62]

Lesser known is the conflict Yogi had with the incomparable Willie Mays, when Yogi was manager of the Mets, By the end of his career some observers believed that Mays had become an insufferable prima donna, although he still enjoyed the near idolatrous affection of the press. Not so with San Francisco sportswriter Glenn Dickey, who wrote a blistering column,

[61] See a full discussion in Barra, 293-298.
[62] See the full account in Barra, 356f, 371ff.

chronicling Mays' horrible treatment of kids, managers, and sportswriters he didn't like. This behavior carried over into his time under Yogi in New York City. In spite of this conflict, and other problems with the Mets, Yogi completed a brilliant year of managing in 1973, taking the club to the World Series, although they lost to the Oakland A's in seven games.

While Yogi's playing career elicits nothing but praise, his managing skills had more mixed reviews. Pitcher Jim Bouton defended Yogi against Billy Martin's assertion that the knowledgeable Berra was a great coach but poor manager because he wasn't mean enough. Bouton replied that while Billy won two pennants by being mean, Yogi won just as many by not being mean. But Bouton does note that although Yogi's Yankee teams liked him, they didn't respect him.[63] Yogi did seem to lose some of his playfulness and spontaneity once he became a manager, probably because a manager is expected to be 100% loyal to the boss rather than to the players, and Yogi just couldn't do that.

Following his illustrious career, Yogi, financially secure and universally loved, enjoyed his retirement years. He was in demand as a speaker, maintained his passion for movies, and often played golf with Stan Musial and other friends.

Off the diamond Yogi is best known for his "Yogi-isms," some of which he said, while others were made up by others. Joe Garagiola,[64] Yogi's life-long friend, insisted that Yogi didn't say funny things, he said things funny. That is, he didn't use the wrong words; he merely put words together in ways nobody ever thought possible. The sayings are not so much clever or

---

[63] Barra, 302, 363. And Tony Castro, *Mickey Mantle: America's Prodigal Son*. .Brassey's, Inc., 2002, 214.

[64] Following Joe Garagiola, *It's Anybody's Ballgame*. Contemporary Books, 1988, Chapter 8. In this entire chapter devoted to Yogi, Garagiola notes that he had never seen Yogi hurt anyone's feelings, being more likely to give himself an ulcer worrying about someone else's feelings.

witty nor a play on words – they were merely his unique way of looking at things. Plus, the real ones made sense in a way. When Yogi was feeling lousy on a bitter cold day, commented, "If a guy can't get sick on a day like today, you ain't healthy." Or,when he warned a radio interviewer, saying "If you ask me something I don't know, I'm not gonna answer." Or when Yogi described how he got along with George Steinbrenner:, he said "It ain't hard. We agree different." Or when he praised radio announcers Mel Allen and Vin Scully: "If they didn't have anything to say, they didn't say it." Or when Casey Stengel asked Yogi what he would do if he found a million dollars, Yogi replied, "If the guy was real poor, I'd give it back to him."

A few of Yogi's most oft-quoted observations include:

* "It ain't over till it's over,"
* "It's déjà vu all over again,"
* "Nobody goes there anymore; it's too crowded."
* "We may be lost, but we're making good time."
* "We made too many wrong mistakes,"
* "When you come to a fork in the road, take it."
* "You got to be very careful if you don't know where you're going because you may not get there."

Following the death of his beloved Carmen in 2014, Yogi's health began to decline. He eventually had to be cared for in a nursing home where he died of natural causes on September 22, 2015. Although he had outlived all those he played with, over a dozen current and former Yankees were among the 400 mourners gathered to celebrate his life at the Church of the Immaculate Conception where Yogi had regularly attended Mass in his adopted hometown of Montclair N.J.[65] Hall of Fame manager Joe Torre was among those who spoke. New York Archbishop Timothy Dolan presided over the service and in his

---

[65] Following the Associated Press report of September 29, 2015.

remarks compared Yogi with Pope Francis, noting they not only shared an "innate courtesy" and exhibited the same smile, the same open face, the same "Aw Shucks" attitude and exciting grasp of life, but that they both had big ears and their families had left Italy in the early 20th century to come to the Americas. Yogi's remains were kept in a simple wooden box topped by a miniature bronze catcher's mitt and placed near the altar until it was carried out by his son Tim and taken to the Gate of Heaven cemetery in nearby East Hanover.

Biographer Barra concludes that Yogi points to something indelibly good in the American character, and he beautifully summarizes Yogi's contribution:

Yogi is more than a living part of our history; he does more than remind us of what once was; he is a symbol of the best of what is, and can still be, of what baseball, the way he played it and lived it, has to tell us. "But it is a game," he once observed, "not life. Although if you play it for money, you can learn a lot about life." That's Yogi, learning us all his experience. That's Yogi: pragmatic, realistic, and playful. That, at its best, is America.[66]

---

[66] Barra, 375.

PART II

"A FEW GOOD MEN"

A lthough the six men in this category played in the years before intense scrutiny into the personal life of public figures, they were nonetheless highly respected by all who came in contact with them. Not flawless, but solid. These were men you would want your daughter to marry. You would gladly have them as guests in your home, and you wouldn't have to worry that they would engage in locker room talk and embarrass your family. They demonstrated that baseball could be an honorable profession.

Wee Willie Keeler
1872-1923
Career: 1892-1910

Willie Keeler was an outfielder who played for the New York Giants, Baltimore Orioles, Brooklyn Dodgers, and New York Yankees. He was elected to the Hall of Fame in 1939.

Born William Henry O'Kelleher in Brooklyn to Irish immigrants, Willie is virtually unknown outside of true baseball aficionados. Those who have heard about him are probably limited to knowing Willie's famous saying regarding the secret of his hitting: "Keep your eye clear and hit 'em where they ain't;

that's all," usually abbreviated to "Hit 'em where they ain't."[67] As John McGraw's biographer, Charles Alexander, has noted, "Baseball has had no more enduring axiom."[68] Keeler was reintroduced to a new generation of fans in 1941 when Willie's 1897 record of hitting safely in forty-four straight games was broken by Joe DiMaggio. Then his name emerged again in 1978 when Pete Rose tied Willie's National League record of forty-four. Keeler's record of eight consecutive two-hundred–hit seasons finally fell when Seattle's Ichiro Suzuki completed ten straight in 2010, although Willie still holds the National League record.[69]

Only 5'4", he was the premier hitter of his day, and with his dazzling speed he roamed the base paths and patrolled the outfield like a much bigger man with longer strides. A true athlete, he was a good boxer and wrestler who surprised people with his strength.

Willie was the poster boy, along with John McGraw and a few others, for "small ball." He was an excellent bunter, and his excellent bat control enabled him to hit the ball to exactly where he wanted it. He is also the player responsible for the significant change in rules in 1901 when foul balls began to be counted as strikes in the National League (the change in the American League occurred in 1903). Furthermore he took advantage of playing at a time when the pitching mound had just been moved to 60'6", and before pitchers could adjust to this substantial change.

Willie's career took off when he joined John McGraw's

---

[67] Cited in Lyle Spatz, *Willie Keeler: From the Playgrounds of Brooklyn to the Hall of Fame.* Rowman and Littlefield, 2015, xv. This is the well-researched definitive biography of Keeler.

[68] Charles Alexander, *John McGraw.* University of Nebraska Press, 1988, 40.

[69] Suzuki developed an interest in baseball history and in Keeler especially as he chased several of Willie's records. As a show of respect he visited Keeler's grave. Spatz, xviii.

Baltimore Orioles in 1894. The Orioles had already established their reputation as being the rowdiest and dirtiest team in baseball. As one sportswriter described them: "The Orioles were by their very nature a raucous, pugnacious crew, sort of an Irish street gang wearing baseball uniforms."[70] The two exceptions on the team were Wilbert Robinson and Keeler. In spite of playing on a bitterly despised team (despised, of course, in every city except Baltimore), these two players were much beloved and respected. Willie didn't fight, didn't argue with umpires, and didn't use foul language, which set him apart from the average player of his day, and certainly set him apart from all of his Orioles teammates. Keeler gained the respect of the brawling McGraw early on when the two of them fought naked in the Baltimore clubhouse shower, following days of McGraw's criticism of Willie's supposed defensive lapses. Teammate Jack Doyle stood guard to prevent interference, and offered 5-4 odds that Keeler wouldn't be the first to give up. As it turned out McGraw indeed was the first to "squeal."[71] Years later, old time umpire Tom Connolly said that Willie was the funniest "little fellow who every walked, and who never said a mean thing to anyone in his life."[72] When asked why he smiled so much, he replied, "Because I get paid for playing baseball."[73]

Keeler was dearly loved by the fans, and he loved them back. Baseball statistician Bill James notes how he would go over to the fence during a break in the game and explain to the kids what was happening in the game, e.g., why a pitching change was being made or why a batter had bunted. This kind of gregariousness made him enormously popular.[74]

---

[70]   Spatz, citing Noel Hynd, 45.

[71]   Cited in Doug Skipper, "Willie Keeler," in *Deadball Stars of the American League*. Potomoc Books, 2006, 708. See also Alexander, 54.

[72]   Cited in Spatz, 87.

[73]   Cited in Skipper, 707.

[74]   Bill James, *The New Bill James Historical Abstract*. Free Press, 2001, 811.

In addition to his favorable public persona, Willie proved adept in the financial world. He became the first $10,000 a year player. Also he was among the first players who engaged in a holdout and spoke articulately about how players were underpaid, noting that players spent the best years of their lives on the diamond when other men spent those years acquiring knowledge and experience that proved lucrative to them later. But ballplayers found themselves at the end of their career unfit to earn considerable money.[75] In addition, living with his father in the house where he was born (his mother died in 1901), Willie made wise investments, primarily in real estate. By 1906 he was probably the wealthiest current player. By 1913 his wealth was estimated to be between $100,000 and $200,000. In today's dollars that would be between $2.5 and $5 million.

Willie proved to be a dapper dresser, wearing only the finest. He also had a fondness for betting on horses, once winning a 100-1 bet.[76] Like many other ball players, he was very superstitious.

Contrary to most players, Willie was kind to rookies and didn't see them as a threat. Also, he was not a drinker or a woman chaser, characteristics that described many of his contemporaries. Furthermore, he maintained a strict regimen during the off-season. He reported to spring training in great condition. He encouraged good eating habits. Cigars were his only vice.

Sadly, Willie began to experience health problems toward the end of his playing career. They only worsened. Breathing difficulties, chest pains, and swelling of the feet and ankles indicated serious heart problems. To make matters worse, his investments declined severely (he was unlucky, not foolish) so that he was in virtual poverty during the last few years of his life. He was forced to sell the family home where he had lived all his

[75] See his lengthy and well-reasoned argument in Spatz, 105f.
[76] His $10 bet won him $1000 in a 1903 race. Spatz, 200.

life and moved into a boardinghouse in the Bedford-Stuyvesant section of Brooklyn. The renter of the house, Clara Roberta Moss, was a single woman five years younger than Willie. Willie and Clara became very close, although the exact nature of their relationship is not known. They may have become only good friends. However, in Willie's last will and testament, drawn up less than two weeks before his death, the lifelong bachelor listed Clara as his sole beneficiary.[77]

Willie's last few years would have been intolerable were it not for the help he received from both the National and American League offices and from his many friends. Virtually all his medical and funeral expenses were paid from funds raised on his behalf.

As the year 1922 was nearing its end, Willie was dying and he knew it. He seemed determined to make it to New Year's Eve and spend it with his close friends. He barely made it, dying around 1:15 a.m. New Year's Day at the age of fifty. His body remained in his apartment in a plain oak casket. Two hundred members of his Elks Lodge visited, with each dropping a red rose in his casket. Former teammates and close friends John McGraw and Hughie Jennings were visibly shaken as they gazed at his remains. Several hundred people gathered outside his apartment in seven inches of snow to witness the casket loaded into the hearse, which proceeded to Our Lady of Good Counsel Catholic Church. Following the service two open cars, filled with flowers, led the funeral procession to Calvary Cemetery in Queens, where Willie was laid to rest in the family plot. Among the eighteen pallbearers were seven former members of the Orioles.

It is common for praise to be heaped in excess following an untimely death, but statements made about Willie seemed heartfelt and appropriate in Keeler's case. Fellow Hall of Famer John McGraw insisted that Willie was the greatest player he

---

[77] Spatz, 293. His estate was worth about $3,500.

ever saw, even outshining Ty Cobb in hitting, fielding, and running. The combative and often mean-spirited McGraw said that Willie was the sweetest man he had ever known. Hall of Famer Sam Crawford not only praised Willie for his exceptional play, but viewed him as nice, very friendly, and always laughing and kidding.[78] New teammate and rookie Jimmy Austin was impressed and surprised when the veteran star Keeler told him that he had a great career ahead of him and if he could be of any help to him, to just say the word.[79] Sportswriter John Foster described him as a perfect gentleman "who did not lose his fine traits in the hurly-burly of the national pastime."[80]

---

[78] Lawrence Ritter, *The Glory of Their Times*. MacMillan, 1966, 53.
[79] *Ibid.*, 74.
[80] Spatz, 304.

Johnny Kling
1875-1947
Career: 1900-1913

John Kling was a catcher who spent most of his career with the Chicago Cubs.

Jews in Germany presented an ugly picture of hatred for many decades. Following one of the periodic anti-Jewish episodes Kling's father, John Kling Sr., fled Germany sometime before 1855 along with many other Jews and found solace in Cincinnati, for some reason a friendly place for Jews who flocked there in large numbers. There in a Unitarian church he married a woman who may or may not have been Jewish. Apparently, many Jews in Cincinnati either became nominal Christians or at least abandoned their Jewish heritage, primarily for social acceptance.

This information is necessary to understand Johnny Kling because his connection with his Jewish heritage was so loose that some even today deny that he was one of the few Jews to play baseball. More on this later.

Unfortunately, this warm welcome for Jews in Cincinnati began to disappear following the Civil War, so John Kling gathered his family and headed west, arriving eventually in Kansas City, Missouri, before Johnny was born in 1875. By age 15, Johnny carried heavy responsibilities in his father's bakery and grocery business. One defining moment for him was when he decided to stop in the middle of his delivery responsibilities to play baseball, which resulted in severe discipline by his father. Johnny's strong sense of business responsibility was born on this day.

Outside of his work in the family business, Johnny spent his time playing baseball and shooting pool. He would soon master both.

He ended up out of necessity becoming a catcher (not his favorite position) as his teams never had a good one. He quickly recognized that the catcher was the most important position on the field, and he possessed the right instincts to develop into a better than average one. He became a first-rate student of the game. Having a really strong throwing arm also helped.

Though quiet by nature, Johnny took on a different persona behind the plate. He was a chatterbox, constantly yelling encouragement to his teammates while trying to distract the batter, engaging him in conversation. Kling soon became known as "Noisy John." The moniker was well deserved. He was always diplomatic and respectful with the home plate umpire, so as to gain an edge on close calls. It seemed to have worked.

By 1903 he was a fixture on the National League club in Chicago (the "Colts" who later became the "Cubs"). He had fallen in love with a Kansas beauty, Lillian May Gradwohl. He had become a very good billiards player. And he had established a reputation as a smart catcher who, unlike many other players, never seemed to get into a fight. In fact, he rarely lost his cool. In 1904 he and Lillian were married in a Jewish synagogue in Kansas City. She was marrying a cleanlliving ball player who didn't smoke, drink, or curse. A rare breed in that era.

His quiet nature prevented him from talking freely with newspaper people, as well as ensuring he didn't showboat on the field or mouth off in the clubhouse. He gained respect, especially from pitchers, for his keen insights into the intricacies of the game. His powers of observation (predating Yogi's famous quip that you could see a lot by looking) were becoming legendary. He seemed to know the strengths and weakness of every batter and could even tell by their stance and the way they held their bat what they were trying to do in every at-bat. He knew who would try to steal and on what pitch. Future Hall of Famer "Three Finger" Brown insisted that he was just an ordinary pitcher until he teamed up with Kling. Brown said that Kling never called a wrong pitch and Brown credited his Hall of Fame status to his catcher. Even the pre-game warmup signaled to Kling what pitch was working best for the pitcher that day. Another Hall of Famer, Walter Johnson, said that Kling was one of the two best catchers ever.[81] "Noisy John" was better known as "Brainy John."

No one was better at throwing out base stealers in his time than Kling. Amazingly, he rarely had to stand up to throw, nailing runners from his squatting position, as well as picking off runners who strayed too far from the bag. His 1546 assists are impressive and are more than eight catchers who are in the Hall of Fame.

Kling's independent streak caused some problems for him during the 1906 season, as the strict, vengeful disciplinarian Frank Chance took over the club. Kling reported late to spring training and raised the ire of Chance, who punished Kling for his insubordination by limiting his playing time. However, Kling still put up good numbers that year.

By the 1907 season, Kling had immersed himself in billiards, as well as opening a billiards parlor. He was financially secure for the first time in his life. He let it be known that he would prefer playing in Cincinnati, angering manager Chance, who benched Kling regularly throughout the season after efforts for a trade to Cincinnati had proven unsuccessful. In spite of less

---

[81]   This information, as well as most of what we know about Kling comes from the definitive biography by Gil Bogen, *Johnny Kling: A Baseball Biography.* McFarland & Co., 2006, 3-4.

playing time, Kling proved to be a key reason the Cubs beat the Tigers in the World Series. Kling stopped Cobb cold on the base paths. Not surprisingly, Chance didn't mention Kling's contributions in his post series interview.

The year 1909 was significant as Kling, the western billiards champion, defeated the eastern champion in a six-night match. This victory enhanced Kling's reputation as a very good baseball player who was also one of the very best pool players in the world. This success in pool, plus his plans to build the most elaborate pool hall in the country, led Kling to announce that he would not play baseball in the coming season. Some observers believed that in addition to these new responsibilities, Kling didn't get along well with Cub owner Charles Murphy and still felt on the outs with Chance. Even though Kling cited his business obligations as the only reason for leaving baseball, he actually decided to organize a minor league team in Kansas City. Interestingly, when it came time in 1909 to divide the 1908 series earnings among the Cub players, Kling was purposely left out even though he had contributed significantly to the Cub's success. Murphy and Chance were getting their revenge.

When Kling expressed interest in returning to the Cubs for the 1910 season, he was hit with the largest fine ($700) in baseball history up to that time for failing to honor his 1909 contract. There is some question as to whether he ever paid the fine.

When the Cubs lost the 1910 World Series to the A's, Chance said publically that Kling allowed the A's to steal his signals. Kling thus became the scapegoat, and most of his teammates refused to speak to him. This is surprising, since Kling had as much as anyone else to do with the Cubs' four championships. There was never any proof that the A's did, in fact, steal the signs. Nonetheless, Kling received a hefty amount of negative publicity following the series. This bad PR would follow him the rest of his life.

Kling came to despise Cub owner Murphy, and was glad to

leave the Cubs, going first to the Boston National's team and then to Cincinnati. Kling had a very high regard and affection for Reds' owner Garry Herrmann, which made Murphy look even worse in contrast.[82]

When Kling left baseball after the 1913 season, he went headlong into successful business ventures. Along with his nephew, Kling built a seven story hotel in Kansas City which would house, on two floors, the most elaborate pool hall in the country. Kling's hall hosted world championship matches. This venture turned out to be a huge moneymaker. Kling opened up restaurants and movie theaters. It was clear that he had a genius for business.

Kling's love of baseball led him to buy a controlling interest in the Kansas City Blues in 1933. Displaying a keen social conscience, one of his most courageous acts was to end segregation at the Blues' ballpark. There is some possibility that the fire that destroyed a theater Kling owned was connected to his refusal to allow segregation at the ballpark. It is known that the Ku Klux Klan was active in that area, and Kling's change of policy was widely publicized. It was a pretty bold move for 1933. Unfortunately, when Kling sold the team in 1937 the "colored" signs went back up, causing considerable bitterness in the black community.

Author Bogen makes an interesting observation near the end of his book. "Johnny Kling was a difficult man to know. Throughout his life, be it in baseball, billiards or business, he established his goals and pursued them with conviction and a firm determination, not easily swayed by arguments contrary to his beliefs. And yet, as difficult as he was to really know, Johnny had the faculty of making friends and holding them. Once the shell around him was broken, he was found to be one of the

---

[82] Bogen describes the many unsavory doings of Murphy in *Ibid.*, 240.

most delightful persons one could meet. He was sugar and spice and everything nice."[83]

Thus, there is somewhat of a mystery about the man. Did anyone really know what he was thinking or feeling? At any rate, he always put his best foot forward in every situation.

Kling seemed to go out of his way to respond to mail requests for signed pictures and signed baseballs, especially from kids, and made a name for himself with his extensive community involvement. At some point he became a Mason.

In the latter part of his life he turned to golf and to farming. He also never failed to respond to the needs of his extended family. He was not a miser with his wealth. He was a devoted husband and a doting father to his two daughters. He also maintained a life-long relationship with his nephew, Bennie Allen, to whom he taught the finer points of billiards.

In an additional effort to maintain a sense of family togetherness, he purchased several units in the Mount Moriah mausoleum for use by his extended family, even having his parents' remains moved there from a nearby cemetery. As a Mason he was eligible to be buried at Mount Moriah, but he went beyond the usual interment and purchased a section in what was called the Temple Mausoleum. It was, and still is, a luxurious and expensive facility with marble throughout. Very few ball players are laid to rest in such an elegant setting. From beginning to end he embodied "family values" long before it was in vogue politically.

A major issue in Gil Bogen's biography has to do with the uncertainty as to whether or not Kling was in fact a Jew. Many of Kling's teammates referred to him "the Jew," and his heritage was not in dispute until a letter from Kling's widow, Lillian, in 1969 declared that Kling was not Jewish, but was rather a Lutheran. Bogen examines in detail the evidence and concludes that Lillian was rewriting Kling's history, because

---

[83] *Ibid.*, 205.

she honestly believed that Kling was being denied entry into the Hall of Fame solely because he was believed to be a Jew. More than anything Lillian wanted to live to see Kling voted into the Hall. The evidence is overwhelming that Kling was Jewish, although obviously he wasn't an observant one.[84]

Cait Murphy points out that being a Jew at Kling's time was no barrier to making it in the game. "Kling [was] a backward example of this: even though he may not have been Jewish, everyone thought he was, and he was one of the most respected players on the Cubs. Barney Dreyfuss, the German-Jewish owner of the Pirates, was generally well-regarded among owners and players.[85]

Bogen also debunks the long-held belief that Kling was the main reason the Cubs lost the 1909 World Series as well as challenging the belief that Kling sat out the 1910 season because he was greedy and wanted more money from Murphy.

Bogen makes a pretty strong case that Kling belongs in the Hall of Fame. Comparing statistics with other HOF catchers, citing assessments of him by his contemporaries (e.g., Evers, Johnson, et.al), and noting that the negative image of him was mostly the result of (1) anti-Semitism, (2) his desegregation of the Blues' ballpark that offended the baseball establishment of his day, and (3) the inaccurate depiction of his 1910 holdout. Bogen concludes that it is time for a reassessment of the best catcher of his time.

Following a trip to Florida in 1946, where he spent time with several baseball buddies from the past (Joe Tinker was probably his best friend from his baseball days), he suffered a heart attack and was admitted to the hospital. About to be released, he suffered a setback and died, aged seventy-one.

In sum, Kling was a brilliant ballplayer and businessman

---

[84] Ibid., 221-233.
[85] Cait Murphy, *Crazy '08: How a Cast of Cranks, Rogues, Boneheads, and Magnates Created the Greatest Year in Baseball History.* Smithsonian Books, 2007, 328f.

who highly valued his family and his community. He was a hard bargainer but also very generous. He was private enough that it remains hard to get inside of his mind and heart to know what he really thought and felt. But from everything we can tell, he was a good man and a solid citizen. He deserves greater recognition for his achievements than he has received.

Herbert Jefferis Pennock
1894-1948
Career: 1912-34

Herb Pennock was a left-handed pitcher who spent his career with the Philadelphia A's, the New York Yankees, and the Boston Red Sox. He was elected to the Hall of Fame a few weeks after his death in 1948.

Herb Pennock was raised in a prominent and highly respected Quaker family in Kennett Square, Pennsylvania, near Philadelphia. He seems to have internalized the Quaker virtues of integrity, truthfulness, simplicity, and respect for all persons.

As a sixth grader he witnessed his first major league game when Connie Mack's A's team defeated the Red Sox. The powerful team of Collins, Waddell, Plank, Bender, et.al left an indelible impression on him. Playing alongside his older brother in high school, he quickly developed a reputation as a smart pitcher. A former major league catcher from his hometown, Mike Grady, taught Pennock how to control and tighten his curveball while he was playing summer ball. This was the pitch that would propel Pennock toward greatness.

A critical decision had to be made following graduation from high school. His family, possessing a deep belief in the importance of education, wanted him to attend the University of Pennsylvania. Herb, on the other hand, was eager to start a career in baseball. Connie Mack's offer proved too hard to resist, and Pennock signed his first contract in May of 1912.

He immediately joined the team and was told by Mack to watch and learn. He did just that and benefited from an immediate friendship with Eddie Collins. In addition, Chief Bender taught Herb how to pitch a screwball. The tall and slender Pennock would never possess an overpowering fastball but would make his fame with an assortment of breaking balls and off-speed pitches. It was said he "had an assortment of curve balls that began with a wrinkle and ended in a jug handle."[86] His career is proof that a sharp mind and outstanding mentors are often key factors in producing a successful pitching career, especially for a player like Pennock who didn't possess an athletic physique.

In the 1915 season, however, with Mack frustrated with his no longer powerhouse club, mistook Pennock's reserved and studious nature as being "dispassionate." An argument in the dugout led to Pennock asking Mack to trade him. Mack did, and Mack would later confess that it was the worst mistake he ever made. Sportswriter Frank Graham said that was one of the most profitable transactions ever engineered by the Yankees or, for that matter, any other club.[87]

A surprising development grew out of his trade to the Red Sox. Pennock quickly became good friends with Babe Ruth. As biographer Keith Craig describes it, "The unlikeliest of companions, the guttersnipe Ruth and the uber-refined

---

[86] Frank Graham, *The New York Yankees: An Informal History.* Southern Illinois Press, 1943, 90.

[87] *Ibid.*, 119.

Pennock became fast friends."[88] As Craig later notes, Ruth's arrogance and insolence never seemed to fray the ties of this lifelong friendship. Pennock probably turned a blind eye to Ruth's many faults, and Herb held to a basic belief that no one should ever be embarrassed or humiliated. One might expect that Herb would occasionally participate in some of the Babe's rampant debauchery, but this is not the case. When Ruth would go off on one of his wild escapades, Pennock would leave. Furthermore, although Herb and the Babe often enjoyed joking with and taking shots at each other, Herb never said a negative word about the Babe to the press, but rather defended him.[89] In fact, Pennock, like others surrounding the Babe were astounded at how Ruth functioned. Pennock describes an occasion when Ruth and his wife ran out of gas one evening and Ruth had to walk five miles to obtain gas. Ruth didn't get to sleep until 5:00 in the morning and then went out to pitch the first game of a doubleheader, winning 1-0, and then won the second game with a homer.[90]

In 1915 Pennock married his childhood sweetheart, Esther Freck. Every indication points to a very strong marriage. She insisted on traveling with him for road games even after the birth of each of their two children. Herb and Esther provided unceasing comfort to and support for each other until the day of Herb's untimely death.

Pennock spent his off seasons putting his good business mind to use as an insurance broker in Philadelphia. His developing business skills would be put to good use when he later became an assistant to Eddie Collins of the Boston Red Sox and the general manager Philadelphia Phillies. In addition, his sensible investments and off-season income enabled

---

[88] Keith Craig, *Herb Pennock: Baseball's Faultless Pitcher.* Rowman and Littlefield, 2016, 33. Much of the information about Pennock in this chapter is culled from this excellent biography.

[89] *Ibid.,*44,68, 232.

[90] Cited in Leigh Montville, *The Big Bam.* Doubleday, 2006, 56.

him to negotiate favorable when it came to signing his yearly contract. He often threatened to quit the game if his demands were not met, and team managements (both Red Sox and Yankees) knew it was no idle bluff. Unlike most players then who possessed few if any skills outside of baseball, Pennock could easily walk away from the game to a life of financial security. Although he rarely received all that he demanded, he commanded substantial raises that few other players could expect. In addition to his off-season employment, he relished the activities of skiing and hunting. The Babe visited most every fall to join Herb in their joint love of hunting.

Pennock's away from the diamond values were regularly exhibited in his love of family, his commitment to the public good, and his accessibility to the press. His friendliness towards all journalists led to their recognition of Herb's solid character and genial disposition. Some of the praise heaped upon him was so excessive as to almost cause embarrassment. One such assessment in *Sporting Life*, even though lengthy, is worth citing:

Pennock represented a new type of ball player, a type that would have curried favor with baseball's founding fathers, who promoted the gentleman's game. He has been an enthusiastic rider of the hounds from earliest boyhood and has had social advantages that few ball players have enjoyed. As a result of this social atmosphere with which his whole home life has been surrounded, and the clean gentlemanly deportment that it has instilled in his nature, Herb Pennock today probably represents the highest type of big-league ball players. Never in his 11-year career has there been a single reflection cast upon his character, never a foul word heard from his lips, never a time when he has lost control of his even, smiling disposition or made any trouble for managers, umpires, or players with whom he has been association – and more than this can be said of no man who has ever graced our national game.[91]

If this isn't baseball sainthood, it's hard to know what is. But it was a sentiment widely shared all through his professional life. He was feted regularly by his hometown and always accepted all the accolades with humility and insistence on giving others credit for his successes. Sportswriters appreciated his thoughtful and respectful comments and his complete cooperation, and thus, as Craig eloquently states, "they heaped encomium atop admiration atop acclaim."[92]

Even the umpires got into the act. Famed umpire Billy Evans, although he described Pennock as frail, said he was a tough bird to beat and that plenty of courage, the will to win, and an ideal temperament surpassed the physicality of a Walter Johnson, Lefty Grove, or Chief Bender.[93]

American League 1925 batting champ Harry Heilmann said that Pennock was not only the greatest pitcher, but also the greatest fellow he knew in baseball.[94] All through his career from every corner the accolades just kept piling up. Teammate Tony Lazzeri said that Pennock was the "greatest money pitcher in the business."[95]

Virtually the only area where Pennock's character might be questioned had to do with integration. When Branch Rickey brought up Jackie Robinson to the Dodgers in 1947, even the saintly Connie Mack severely criticized Rickey and said he lost respect for him. Pennock made no critical comments about this radical development in baseball, but as the Phillies general manager he had hired his old friend Ben Chapman as

[91] Cited in Craig, 60.
[92] *Ibid.*, 68. Webster defines encomium as "glowing and warmly enthusiastic praise."
[93] *Ibid.*, 74.
[94] *Ibid.*, 87.
[95] Cited in William A. Cook, *Waite Hoyt: A Biography of the Yankees' Schoolboy Wonder.* McFarland & Co., 2004, 95.

manager. The Alabama native Chapman proved to be the most vicious harasser of Robinson, shouting things at Robinson that even caused some discomfort among his players. In spite of pressure from the Commissioner's office, Pennock stuck by his old friend who he admired for his baseball savvy.

Where things became nasty at this point was when sportswriter Harold Parrott wrote in his book *The Lords of Baseball* that he was once in Branch Rickey's office when Pennock called Rickey to tell him, "Just can't bring the Nigger here with the rest of your team, Branch. . .We're just not ready for that sort of thing yet. We won't be able to take the field against your Brooklyn team in that boy Robinson is in uniform."

Biographer Craig goes to great length to examine this matter, citing several reasons why that conversation most likely didn't happen. The comment goes against everything we know about Pennock's character, including Pennock's family's great affection for one Florence "Gig" Simon, a black woman that Pennock provided refuge for when she fled from her abusive husband, and who, in fact, became a beloved member of the Pennock household and helped raise the children. When "Gig" died at the ripe old age of 107, she was buried in the Pennock plot.

Craig casts serious doubt as to Parrott's veracity, while admitting that even though Pennock questioned the wisdom of Rickey's experiment, Pennock would never have uttered such an inflammatory statement. Furthermore, Craig quotes a friend of the Pennock family, Crow Mattson, who swore that Pennock was not a racist, and, in fact, had mentioned to Mattson in a conversation that Jackie was good for baseball, and that there were other very good black players who deserved a chance.[96]

It is worth noting that in the 1990s Kenneth Square was planning to erect a statue of its favorite son, but the project has never seen fruition. It is believed that the hint of racism in

---

[96] See the lengthy discussion of this matter in Craig, 201-211.

Pennock's otherwise impeccable character is the main reason the tribute has been derailed.[97]

Following his playing days, Pennock devoted his energies to developing players, first with the Red Sox and then as general manager of the Philadelphia Phillies. Following the pattern perfected by Branch Rickey, Pennock set out to develop a farm system that would make the Phillies into a powerhouse. He had the full support of owner Robert Carpenter, Jr. to sign and develop prospects who would later be known as the "Whiz Kids." Unfortunately, Pennock didn't live to see this happen. While in New York City with Carpenter for the winter baseball meetings, Pennock complained of a headache, but nonetheless headed with Carpenter to the Waldorf Astoria for a meeting. Upon entering the revolving doors Pennock raised his hand to his head saying, "There's that headache again," and immediately collapsed to the floor. Sometime earlier an artery had burst in his brain and the pooling blood cut off the oxygen supply. He was rushed to the hospital a mere two blocks away but was pronounced death within an hour. Some survive cerebral hemorrhages today, but not in 1948.

The baseball world reacted quickly, heaping praise befitting a saint. It was said that there was not a better liked man in sports, and that he was as fine a character as the game had ever known. Dan Dailey of the *New York Times* said that Pennock was a humble man in the presence of his own pitching greatness who was at home jousting with the "mugs" of the game as he was holding intelligent conversation in a drawing room.[98] Other papers noted that there was not a mean half ounce of blood in his veins. The Babe, who died six months later, declared that everyone was crazy about Herb, and that he had never made an enemy in his life.

Commission Happy Chandler wanted to have a large

---

[97] *Ibid.*, 252.

[98] *Ibid.*, 242f.

delegation of baseball dignitaries attend the funeral, but Esther asked him to forego such a plan and allow the family to grieve in private. Chandler complied. Esther did consent to Kennett Square's request for a public wake in the American Legion Hall (Pennock was a World War I veteran). More than 3000 showed up to pay their respects.

Tributes continued to pour in, but probably the most eloquent one came from the president of the minor league's American Association, Bruce Dudley. It deserves to be quoted in full:

Herb Pennock was the most genuinely beloved personage ever connected with the sport of baseball. There is no exception. Actually, I cannot think of any person who approaches Herb for universal lovability, not only in the baseball world, but in every circle penetrated by his personality of graciousness, wholesomeness, and considerateness.

Herb was as easy to meet as a shoeshine boy, and he was as courteous to and as considerate of a shoeshine boy as he was considerate of and as courteous to all other mortals with whom he came in contact. With Herb, there was no rich or poor, no black or white, no Jew or Gentile, no Catholic or Protestant. They were all human beings, and Herb was gracious to all of them, and all of them adored him.

Herb never had the faintest intimation of what an exceptional person he was. He would have just as beloved and just as revered had he been a bus driver or dentist.

Sometimes I think the Lord must have granted this world the few years it had of Herb Pennock to show that it is possible for the same person to be great and to be human.[99]

Although our purpose is to examine the personal life of Herb Pennock, a few notable things about his baseball career deserve mention.

Arguably his best pitching performance ever was in the celebrated fifteen inning duel with Lefty Grove with Pennock

---

[99] Cited in Craig, 255.

coming out on top 1-0. Grove, by the way, said that there were only pitchers in baseball who wouldn't throw at a batter: Walter Johnson and Herb Pennock.[100] Not surprisingly, these two are among a tiny few who achieved baseball sainthood.

After the 1925 disastrous season for the Yankees, Pennock seriously considered retiring as it was said that the Yankees had no regard for training and that the team's best double play have been a shot of bourbon chased by a beer.

Herb was a notoriously slow worker on the mound, fidgeting around between pitches, much to the dismay of the batter. Manager Joe McCarthy told Pennock that Mrs. McCarthy referred to him as her "noodle pitcher." Was this because of his deliberate manner on the mound? No, it was because by the time he began his windup until he released the ball she could have prepared a mess of noodles.

When Pennock began to develop arm problems he resorted to any number of quackish cures such as having a teammate paint stripes across his chest with some sort of liniment and hiring a beekeeper to place a hive of bees on his arm in hopes that the bee venom would cure his neuritis. There is no indication that the desired results were achieved.

His election to the Hall of Fame, along with Pie Traynor, a mere two weeks after his death raised some eyebrows, causing some to claim that his election was a sympathetic vote. However, the vote was taken in December, and Pennock died in January. Esther described the vote as more a sentimental vote.

---

[100] Cited in Henry W. Thomas, *Walter Johnson: Baseball's Big Train.* University of Nebraska Press, 1995, 95.

Francis Joseph "Lefty" O'Doul
1897-1969
Career: Player: 1919-20, 22-23, 28-34
PCL Manager: 1935-1957

Lefty O'Doul played for several major league teams but had his best years with the Dodgers and Phillies. His long career as a manager in the Pacific Coast League made him a well known and much beloved figure in California, and especially in San Francisco.

Lefty O'Doul has not been given serious consideration for the Hall of Fame, primarily due to his short career and the fact that he was a very poor fielder (Said one sportswriter: "O'Doul could run like a deer. Unfortunately, he threw like one, too"). But as a hitter he excelled during a seven year span from 1928 to 1934. He won two National League batting crowns and had a record 254 hits during the 1929 season, a record that still stands in the National League. Only two American Leaguers, George Sisler with 257 in 1920 and Ichiro Suzuki with 262 in 2004 have bested O'Doul's feat. There are still those who think he belongs in the Hall, pointing out that several in the Hall had short careers (e.g., Dizzy Dean, Sandy Koufax), and that his hitting statistics compare favorably with several players who have been inducted.

But the concern of our study is not what happened on the diamond, but what kind of a person a player was. We don't know a great deal about Lefty, but there are some characteristics that stand out.

Born and raised in San Francisco, he would become the most beloved player from that city, even surpassing the great Joe DiMaggio. Of course, a major reason for this is that Lefty played and managed in the city for many years, apparently refusing to consider a major league appointment because of his love for and dedication to his hometown. He built up a lot of goodwill over the course of his years there.

But it was not just his playing and managing ability that endeared him to the city. He genuinely liked to be around people, and never met a stranger. While walking the streets, he would stop and chat with numerous people on the way to his destination, often remembering their names, but frustrating those walking with him who were ready to move on. Everybody who came in contact with him experienced him as an extremely friendly person who took an interest in them. He truly possessed the gift of gab.

He was also a fun loving guy. Even his epitaph includes this characteristic because it states in large letters that "He was here at a good time and had a good time while he was here." In fact, some believed that he overdid it to the extent that it shortened his career. One sportswriter concluded that Lefty "overworked his arm trying to make good as a pitcher and under worked the old egg in his hours of leisure. Boon companions and sudden fame tagged him out."[101]

---

[101] Cited in Richard Leutzinger, *Lefty O'Doul: The Legend that Baseball Nearly Forgot.* Camel Bay Publishing Group, 1997, 32. Leutzinger's brief work pulls together most of what we know about O'Doul.

One such occasion shows both Lefty's generosity and humor. Someone had written a check at a bar supposedly signed by O'Doul that had bounced. Upon checking it out it was evident that the signature on the check was not O'Doul's, and the bar owner admitted that he had never met Lefty. But surprisingly, Lefty plopped down a $20 bill to cover the charges and then told the bartender that "the next time someone comes in and says that he's me, take him out in back and have somebody hit a few balls to him. If he catches them, you know he's a phony."[102] O'Doul confessed that he was no angel, and he fit the Irish stereotype of heavy drinking. Apparently he did not become belligerent when drinking, but still remained a friendly guy who could relate to anyone. Like many others, he found ways to secure ample booze during the period of Prohibition and continued that lifestyle to his dying day.

We are not sure how his lifestyle affected his marriages. He was married to his first wife, Abbie, for twenty-nine years before they divorced and then very shortly afterwards married a longtime girlfriend, Jean, in 1953, who was twenty-four years his junior. Neither marriage produced any off-spring, although Jean had a son by a previous marriage that Lefty never quite connected with. Players' private lives, as we have seen throughout our study, were pretty much left alone by the press unless the behavior was so grievous that it made headlines. O'Doul's private activities never reached that level, so it is not known if he engaged in semi-affairs or one-night stands as many players have done. If he did, he was certainly discreet.

O'Doul's love of children reached near epic proportions. He was generous to a fault with kids. He even went so far as to toss baseballs to kids during games (when that wasn't done in those days) and carried an ample supply of balls and bats in his car to hand out to kids everywhere. He never turned down autographs and treated all children with respect. Not all

---

[102] *Ibid.*, 26.

players did that. He would stop what he was doing to carry on a conversation with a young boy. At times he was known to impulsively give all the money he had with him to some kid or a group of kids. On one such occasion when he was being honored at Candlestick Park with a check of $1,500, he immediately turned it over to the Police Athletic League to buy equipment for underprivileged boys.

In general, money meant very little to him, and though he was paid well as a player and especially as a manager, he appeared totally devoid of greed. He said once that he loved the game so much that he would have played for nothing and always accepted management's offer without complaint. And, as we have seen, he had a penchant for giving away a lot of his money. An aspect not widely known about O'Doul was his major involvement in Japan following the war. Although he didn't introduce baseball to Japan (that was done by a missionary in 1873), he is still recognized as the Father of Baseball in that country. He made numerous trips to Japan, sometimes alone and sometimes with other players, and spent a large amount of time and resources helping the Japanese understand and play the game properly. An example of his generosity not associated with baseball occurred in 1951 when he donated the equivalent of nearly $3000 to a Tokyo school for the mentally handicapped. General MacArthur went so far as to say that O'Doul did what diplomats would not have been able to do when he in essence laid a foundation for friendship between the U.S. and Japan. MacArthur's successor, General Matthew Ridgeway, agreed with MacArthur's assessment in saying that "Words cannot describe Lefty's wonderful contributions through baseball to the post-war rebuilding effort." This is mighty high praise coming from men who weren't known for showering others with plaudits.

In many ways O'Doul saw himself as a teacher, and his players viewed him in the same light. Both Joe and Dom DiMaggio, Ted Williams, and Ferris Fain, all outstanding hitters, credit O'Doul with much of their success. (Lefty and his wife were one of the few invited to Joe's wedding to Marilyn Monroe). O'Doul spent hours in Japan teaching the fine points of hitting to aspiring players. He worked tirelessly with young kids on the fundamentals of hitting. But even here, his humor could come to the fore. Once seeing a player trying out for the Seals having trouble catching fly balls, he offered to demonstrate the correct way. He dropped the first ball hit to him, turned to the aspiring player and said, "You've got left field so fucked up now, nobody can catch anything out here."[103]

He didn't hesitate to share his philosophy of managing. He believed the key to good managing was keeping his players happy, because the technical and fundamental aspects of the game were known by all. "Somebody has to be in charge, but what I'm saying is this: the difference between a winning manager and a losing manager is about five percent, if they both have teams of equal ability. The small difference is in guessing right, in intuition. Guessing when to yank a pitcher, guessing when to put in the right pinch hitter. Even then it's mostly luck. I win some games on intuition - about one percent of the five percent. In the long-run, the five percent edge comes from knowing your players, knowing their personal problems, getting next to them so they put out for you, and keeping discipline, but not like a cop. A team needs a manager like Boy Scouts need a scout master. Somebody has to be in charge."[104]

Although he took the game very seriously, he didn't take himself so seriously that he couldn't cut up a bit during games. Once after a prolonged slump, he got a base hit, tipped his cap to the base, and dropped to his knees to plant a kiss on the bag. At another time he was protesting a fine he had received from the League office for arguing with an umpire. O'Doul went into the stands to secure the name of twenty witnesses who would

[103] *Ibid.*, 26.
[104] *Ibid.*, 104.

back up his side of the story. Later as San Francisco Seals manager he carried a big red handkerchief in his hip pocket, which he would wave at the opposing pitcher in an attempt to unsettle him. Seals fans quickly picked up on this habit and brought red handkerchiefs to the game to join in the fun.

O'Doul possessed other quirks. Baseball players are notorious among athletes for being superstitious, but O'Doul outdid most. He always (yes always) put on his left shoe before putting on his right shoe. He had "lucky lockers" at each ballpark that he insisted no other player could use. He would leave a shirt or tie hanging on a door knob at his home, and his wife knew never to move it.

During his playing days he was known as the best golfer in the National League, shooting in the 70s. He also was a gifted amateur photographer, even taking movie shots during his world travels.[105]

O'Doul, being the Irishman he was, wore green religiously. This is attested on his gravestone as "The Man in the Green Suit," along with the aforementioned reference to having a good time. He started wearing green almost exclusively (even, it is said, green underwear) in 1929, following a torrid hitting streak and he never abandoned the habit. His wardrobe certainly didn't clash with his green eyes.

O'Doul suffered a stroke on November 12, 1969, but hung on until a massive coronary blockage did him in on December 7th. A large number of people showed up for his funeral at St. Edward the Confessor Roman Catholic Church in San Francisco. Notables in attendance included Joe DiMaggio, who had been mentored by O'Doul while still in the minors, Joe Cronin, President of the American League, and Charles Feeney, President of the National League.

O'Doul was basically a decent man who cared about others

---

[105] Harold Johnson (ed.), *Who's Who in Major League Baseball*. Buxton Publishing, 1933, 303.

and who was generous in sharing all that he had, whether knowledge or finances. It is easy to see why he was a most beloved figure in San Francisco.

O'Doul trivia:
* He was taught how to play ball by a woman. Rosie Stultz was Lefty's 7th grade teacher and coach, and taught him the fundamentals of the game.
* During his wasted years as an aspiring pitcher he holds the record for giving up the most runs in one inning, 13, in a game against the Red Sox in 1923.
* Although a consummate Irishman, he actually carried some "French genes" as well. His Irish grandmother married a Frenchman named Odoul, but she insisted on adding the apostrophe and had their name legally changed to O'Doul.

Al Lopez
1908-2005
Career: Player: 1928-1947; Mgr.: 1951-1969

Alfonso Ramon Lopez was a catcher who played for Brooklyn, Boston (Braves), and Pittsburg. He achieved his fame as manager of the Cleveland Indians and the Chicago White Sox. He was elected to the Hall of Fame in 1977.

As ballplayers go, Al Lopez had an unusual ethnic background. His parents had immigrated from Spain to Cuba in the mid 1890s, but then moved to Tampa, Florida in the early 1900s to join 10,000 other workers in the many cigar factories in that area. Before long they would give birth to their 8th child, Al. Although many major leaguers were raised in the Tampa area, Lopez was the lone Hispanic to make it to the big leagues. (The Cuban Dolf Luque was the first Latin to become a big league star). Lopez thus came to symbolize the path to success for many Latins in the Ybor City district of Tampa.

His childhood days in his close-knit family in Ybor City were good ones. The Spanish, Cuban, and Italian neighborhoods seemed to get along very well. Early on, Al fell in love with baseball and spent most of his time on the sandlots. As he worked his way through the minor league system, he experienced his share of racist name calling (e.g., "Cuban Nigger," etc.), but it didn't seem to affect him in any significant way. He viewed bench-jockeying and riling others as simply a part of the game so he didn't take it personally. He impressed all with his spirited play on the diamond. His pleasant, easy-going disposition won him respect from all he encountered on and off the field.

Although Lopez made brief appearances with the Brooklyn Dodgers in the 1928 and 1929 seasons, by 1930 he had become a fixture on the team, mostly as a catcher. He was fortunate to learn a great deal from the much-loved manager Wilbert Robinson during his early seasons when he spent most of time on the bench. In 1934, Casey Stengel became manager of the Dodgers and he and Lopez forged a deep friendship that would last a lifetime. Though gregarious and humorous Stengel was about as opposite to the quiet, business-like demeanor of Lopez as one could be, they got along beautifully. Thus the combination of Lopez's instinctive skill in handling pitchers, along with the tutelage he received from future Hall of Famers Robinson and Stengel, promoted his growing reputation as that of a baseball guru. Interestingly, the close friendship between Lopez and Stengel was not diminished despite the fact that Casey traded Lopez, not once, but twice, to other teams.

After being traded to Boston, in 1936, along with his closest friend, Tony Cuccinello, he met Evelyn "Connie" Kearney, a dancer in New York City. They married in 1939; and a year later their only child, Alfonso Ramon Lopez, Jr., now a lawyer in

Tampa was born[106] The marriage was a happy one, and Lopez enjoyed being a father. He never pushed his son into sports, but rather stressed the importance of education along with the duty to live within a code of right and wrong, and of the necessity of being kind to all people.[107]

Because of his age and family obligations, Lopez wasn't called to serve in the military during World War II, unlike many other players of his generation. No one, however, ever questioned his patriotism.

Lopez's cautious nature was revealed in the 1946 effort by some to form a players' union. Although Lopez clearly inherited from his father a strong pro-union bias (stemming from his father's involvement in the cigar-making union), he voted against a walk-out by his Pirate team, believing that a substantial number of other teams should join them before attempting a strike. The percentages were not with a lone walk-out, and Lopez was "a percentage man," on and off the field.

Lopez's reputation of decency and serenity led Bill Veeck to state that if Lopez had a weakness as a manager, it was that he was *too* decent. The image of a successful manager in the minds of many baseball people was that of John McGraw or Leo Durocher, hard-driving and merciless to friend and foe alike. Lopez's image was more like that of his mentor Wilbert Robinson, but Lopez possessed a desire to win that was second to none. Burning beneath that quiet professionalism was a hatred of losing. Losses led to insomnia and stomach

---

[106] This writer wrote to Al, Jr., to ask for a phone or email interview to enquire about his father's relationships with his wife and with their children and to find out how his father and friend Tony Cuccinello decided to be buried next to each other. Mr. Lopez did not respond. For whatever reason, Lopez's biographer, Wes Singletary chose not to delve into Lopez's personal life.

[107] Interviews with Al, Jr., can be found in the definitive biography on Lopez by Wes Singletary, *Al Lopez: The Life of Baseball's El Senor.* McFarland & Co., 1999. See especially p. 100. Much of the information in this essay is found in this very good work.

aches. He couldn't leave the game at the park but mulled over losses even at home. Baseball was not just a job. It was his life.

He rarely complimented players, but he also never scolded or rebuked them in front of others. He didn't fine players for making mistakes; he would just bench them, especially for mental mistakes or for lack of hustle.

As a manager he had three basic rules: always throw to the cutoff man, always round first base on a single when a teammate is trying to score, and keep the curfew. He also believed that a manager could contribute two basic things to a club: inspire the players and handle the pitchers properly. He excelled in both of these. He tried to keep thing simple and to allow his players the freedom to play their game. Instead of a rigid formula, he sought to adapt his strategy to the material he had on the team A good example of this skill was the way he fashioned the "Go-Go" Chicago White Sox. His team succeeded in outscoring their opponents by speed and smart baserunning, solid defense, and crafty pitching. His achievement of leading the seemingly inferior talented Sox to the 1959 World Series has become legendary.

An important part of Lopez's success was his ability to hire and keep good coaches. His best friend Tony Cuccinello topped the list; Don Gutteridge was another.

Lopez clearly had difficulty reacting to the changes in the game in the 1960s. He had been nurtured in an era when the team was everything, and players sacrificed their own ambitions for the sake of the team. He couldn't communicate as well with the new breed of players who were concerned about their personal freedom, and about issues of race and economics. To them team unity and the welfare of the whole team became secondary to personal goals. In addition, in contrast to players of Lopez's day, the newer players often refused to play when dealing with seemingly minor ailments or injuries. As had been the case of several other successful managers, the game seemed to have passed him by. Lopez realized that he was no longer a good fit, so he left the game in 1965 at age fifty-seven. A brief return to managing in 1968-9 proved unsuccessful.

Lopez's biographer, Wes Singletary, was obviously smitten with this good man and highlights Lopez's many good points. The area which caused Singletary the most concern had to do with the charge that Lopez was prejudiced, if not racist. Hall of Famer Larry Doby was the most outspoken player who insisted that Lopez was prejudiced against blacks. After interviewing several players and other observers, Singletary concludes that Lopez was not a racist, but that he failed to be sensitive to what black players were experiencing on and off the diamond. Lopez didn't sees ribbing and bench-jockeying as racist, but as a part of the game. Furthermore, his failure to communicate well with black players was his general way of relating to all players. He communicated through his coaches and thus seemed distant to many of his players, and blacks often interpreted this differently than did whites. Singletary cites other players, both black and white, who defend Lopez against charges of racism. While trying his best to defend Lopez's integrity and legacy, Singletary admits that for various reasons, Lopez couldn't sympathize with the way blacks were treated in the game, and in society as a whole. Of course, this was true for many in baseball and for many in American society during those tumultuous times. They just didn't get it. But having said this, Singletary points out that Doby couldn't cite proof for some of his allegations, and that several other responsible observers shared Lopez's assessment that Doby failed to live up to his potential. In light of that, Doby shouldn't lay all the blame for this on a racist society.[108]

Following retirement, Lopez spent the bulk of his time on the golf course, where he often "shot his own age;" but

---

[108] http://usatoday30.usatoday.com/sports/baseball/2005-10-30allopez-obit_x.htm

he maintained an interest in baseball via television. His wife Connie died in 1983, and Lopez never remarried. Although widowed for more than twenty years, he didn't suffer the long, sad, agonizing declines that so many elderly people do.

Lopez's humility is seen in a 1994 interview when a ballpark in Tampa was named after him, and a statue was erected in his honor. Lopez's response was, "Why are you doing this? I was just doing something I liked."[109]

In that same interview, Lopez recalled that he was thrown out of an exhibition game in Tampa after umpire John Stevens blew a call on the first day of spring training. "I hollered, 'John, are you going to start out the year like that? First play we have, and you miss it. Are we going to have to put up with you all spring?'" Stevens responded that one more word out of Lopez and he would be tossed out of the game. Lopez yelled, "You can't throw me out of this ballpark. This is my ballpark – Al Lopez Field. Stevens said, 'Get out of here.' He threw me out of my own ballpark!"

Lopez suffered a heart attack on October 29, 2005 and died two days later at the ripe old age of ninety-seven. It is noteworthy that his place in the mausoleum is right next to that of his friend Tony Cuccinello, who died in 1995.

In assessing Lopez's life, it is clear that he ranks right up there with the really good guys of the game. Singletary concludes his book by summarizing Lopez's character: "Avoid the distractions, keep to the basics, come to work, and compete. These were the traits that Lopez personified as a player and manager and continues by example to embody today. In this resolute fashion he remains yesterday's understated diamond gentleman, El Senor."[110]

[109] *Ibid.*
[110] *Ibid.*, 232

Richie Ashburn
1927-1997
Career: 1948-1962

Don Richard Ashburn was a center-fielder for the Philadelphia Phillies. He was voted into the Hall of Fame in 1995. He was also a much beloved radio announcer for Phillies games following his playing career.

Born in the small town of Tilden, Nebraska, Richie, in many ways, remained a small town boy all his life. Raised in a solid, loving mid-western family, he would maintain those values throughout his life.[111]

Early on it was obvious that "Whitey" (his nickname due to his striking blond hair) possessed great athletic skills and could have played professionally in several other sports. His two greatest assets were his speed and his strong desire to win. While many athletes claim to give a 100% all the time, Richie

---

[111] Most of the information in this chapter is culled from Fran Zimniuch, *Richie Ashburn Remembered.* Sports Publishing L.L.C., 2005.

really did it. He was a vital part of the famous "Whiz Kids" who made it to the World Series in 1950.

Richie's upbringing made him uncomfortable with the way players treated Jackie Robinson after Robinson broke the racial barrier. Richie is credited with helping to put an end to the abuse against Jackie from the Phillies dugout. He later apologized to Jackie for the abuse he suffered from his Philly teammates. It's not that Richie didn't razz opposing players. His competitive nature meant that he would do everything he could to disrupt the concentration of an opposing pitcher. He was especially verbal when it came to spitball pitchers like Lew Burdette. Once after grounding out against Burdette, he yelled that next time he would try to hit the dry side of the ball.

He also let umpires know when he thought they had missed a call, although he would often do it in a humorous way. One funny incident occurred when Richie played in spite of having a bad case of intestinal flu. While sprinting from first to third on a hit to the outfield, the bug got the better of him when he had an "accident" when sliding into third. Umpire Ken Burkhart took a look at Richie and said, "Richie, you just crapped in your pants." Richie looked up and replied, "Kenny, that's the best call you've made all year!" Burkhart tossed him out of the game and sent Richie to a much- needed shower.

Richie had the rare distinction of hitting the same person twice with a foul ball. A Mrs. Roth was hit in the face with a foul ball and while she was being removed from the stands on a stretcher another foul from Richie's bat found her. Consistent with his character he later visited her in the hospital.

Richie's adeptness at fouling off pitches until he got the pitch he wanted led teammate Jim Brewer to ask that Richie foul a pitch in the direction of Brewer's wife, with whom Brewer was experiencing martial problems. During a game a foul ball from Richie came very close to her. Brewer stuck his head out of the dugout and yelled, "Two feet to the right and you've got her."

Like all other players of his era, Richie bristled at the way management possessed complete control over the players, often determining salary arbitrarily; completely unrelated to a player's accomplishments. After the 1958 season, when Richie beat Willie Mays for the batting title with a .350 average, he was sent a contract with a $2,500 cut with the explanation "You didn't hit your singles far enough." Richie responded that if he had hit them any farther, they would have been outs! The humor failed to get him more money.

Ashburn's humor is one of his defining characteristics. He had a wonderful ability to poke fun at himself and others. Humor, combined with humility, endeared him to all players with whom he came into contact. He also went beyond what most players did when it came to signing autographs. He would remain until everyone seeking an autograph got one.

Ashburn could also charm the socks off most anyone. People in all walks of life remarked how comfortable they felt in his presence.

It was natural for Richie to move to the broadcasting booth following his remarkable career. He possessed the rare ability to make listeners feel he was talking directly to them. His quick wit enlivened a broadcast. Once, when a player brought back some of the ash from the Mount St. Helens eruption, someone in the booth began to discuss the various properties of ash, and how the ash near the explosion was finer than the ash from the other side of the mountain. Ashburn deadpanned, "I think if you've seen one piece of ash, you've seen them all."

Ashburn tried to downplay the fact that he was passed over for the Hall of Fame for fifteen years before the Veterans Committee voted him in. In 1983 he joked that since he had been in broadcasting as well as writing regularly about baseball, he stood an excellent chance of being the only man rejected by the Hall of Fame in three different categories.

Those who knew him well, however, knew that it hurt him that he regularly came up short in the voting when his credentials compared favorably with many already enshrined. A vigorous campaign by long-time fan Jim Donahue finally bore fruit, and he entered the hallowed Hall with another Phillie, Mike Schmidt, in 1995.

Much of Ashburn's life revolved around his family. He met his future wife, Herberta "Herbie" Cox at Norfolk Junior College and proposed her after only a few dates. Their union produced six children, and Richie bemoaned the fact that he had not been present for the births of any of them due to his life in baseball. Due to lengthy absences from home, baseball places a huge strain on the best of marriages, but Herbie was very adept at organizing and caring for a large family. It is clear that Richie dearly loved his children and was involved in their lives as much as he could be. He later proved to be a model grandfather.

It is a puzzle that after twenty-eight years of marriage Richie and Herbie separated. They never divorced and the entire family still gathered together on important occasions and celebrated like nothing had changed. If there was another woman in Richie's life no one has mentioned it. The children simply took the explanation that although their parents still loved each other they could no longer live together. They remained close friends and Herbie even brought the family to spring training in Florida often. This unusual arrangement didn't seem awkward to them or to their friends.

In 1987, ten years after the separation, their second child, Jan, was killed in an automobile accident. This was the saddest day of Ashburn's life and both his family and friends said that Richie never got over it.

Richie immensely enjoyed his work as a radio commentator for Phillies games. His dry wit and his vast knowledge of the game made him a beloved figure in Philadelphia. His best friend was broadcast partner Harry Kalas.

Following a game with the Mets at Shea Stadium Ashburn retired to his hotel room in Manhattan. Early the following morning, September 9, 1997, Richie called the Phillies traveling secretary to report that he was ill. Hotel security was informed and found Richie dead of a heart attack. Smoking and diabetes probably contributed to the unexpected death of one who seemed so vital and vigorous. The deep affection in which he was held is seen in the fact that more than 40,000 people walked past his casket. One looks in vain to find a negative comment about him.

Following the funeral service people were waiting in line as far as the eye could see to pay their respects to the family. "On that sad day in Philadelphia, Ashburn's family did exactly what they knew he would have done in a similar circumstance. They stayed and greeted every person who waited in line to pay their respects. It is the Ashburn way."[112]

His son, Richard Jr., later established The Richie Ashburn Baseball Foundation to provide free baseball camps for Philadelphia area kids where life skills, as well as baseball skills, are emphasized. The Foundation also assists in finding academic scholarships.

Richie was somewhat the Yogi Berra of Philadelphia with his humorous quips. Included are such remarks as:

"Houston is the only town where women wear insect repellent instead of perfume."

"The kid doesn't chew tobacco, smoke, drink, curse, or chase broads. I don't see how he can possibly make it."

"You can bet the house on it. This is a lead-pipe cinch bunting situation."

"In my 15 years of eligibility under the Baseball Writers Association, my center field opposition consisted of Willie Mays, Duke Snider and Mickey Mantle. Hard to believe I didn't make it against those turkeys."

---

[112] *Ibid.*, 99.

"He looks a little runnerish, Harry."

"Right down the middle for a ball."

"Boys, this game looks a lot easier from up here (in the broadcasting booth)."

PART III

"LIFE ISN'T FAIR"

This is section comprises the sad part of the book. It can be sad for different reasons. Obviously an early death is tragic. But life's circumstances often bring seemingly excessive hardships to some while skipping over others. Sometimes a single moral lapse can ruin an otherwise honorable life. Sometimes no good deed goes unpunished. Sometimes public figures can be hounded by the press until their lives become miserable.

There are a broad range of reasons for placing these seven players in in this category. Several of these men could have been placed in the Few Good Men category, but they had to deal with enough adversity to warrant looking at them from a different angle.

Addie Joss
1880-1911
Career:1902-1910

Adrian "Addie" Joss was a right-handed pitcher who spent his brief career with the Cleveland Bluebirds (later Naps before eventually becoming the Indians). He was elected to the Hall of Fame in 1978.

For someone who died a hundred years ago after a short life of 31 years, it is not easy to gather a great deal of information. But baseball historian Scott Longert has discovered enough to give us an idea of what this man was like and shares it in an overdue, if brief book.[113] Little has been written about Joss as a human being outside of this book.

Adrian Joss was born in Wisconsin, the only child of Swiss emigrants Jacob and Theresa Joss. Jacob amassed a fortune making cheese but died at age 37 of liver disease brought on by alcohol abuse,and left his wife and son in dire straits financially.

---

[113] Scott Longert, *Addie Joss: King of the Pitchers.* SABR, 1998.

Theresa's skills as a seamstress and dressmaker, however, kept the family clothed and fed.

One thing his father bequeathed Addie was a kind demeanor. Addie was warm and friendly as a youth and charmed people from the moment they met him. People were always at ease in his presence.

This tall, lanky kid with long arms fell in love with baseball at a young age and wanted to do little else besides firing a ball at a batter. Following grade school, he attended Wayland Academy, which was affiliated with the University of Chicago. There he received a good education and developed his unique pitching style. Like Luis Tiant later, Joss would twist to face second base before whirling around to throw sidearm. Also, like later Hall of Famer Dennis Eckersley, Joss seemed like all arms and legs to batters who had trouble picking up the ball. He would later become arguably the best fielding pitcher in the game but would also be among the worst hitters in the league.

While at Wayland he became certified to teach (at age 16!) But his heart was in baseball and he left the teaching profession forever to accept a scholarship at Sacred Heart College where he studied civil engineering. Contrary to stories that circulated for years that Joss attended, even graduated, from the University of Wisconsin, there is no evidence for this whatsoever.

His first professional contract was in 1900 with the Toledo Mud Hens where he enjoyed immediate success and where he met his future wife Lillian Shinavar. They would eventually make their permanent home there. While in the Western Association he had a memorable duel with future Hall of Famer and nutcase Rube Waddell. Their paths would cross again in the big leagues.

Joss' entry into the major leagues came with the American League Cleveland Bluebirds where he would remain for his entire nine-year career. The team was later called the Naps after their celebrated player/manager Nap Lajoie. The 6'3" 185 lb. Joss was immediately given the nickname "The Human

Slat." "Stick," "Signpost," and "Hairpin" were other names given to him by later teammates. His affable and easy-going nature won him admiration from both players and fans. Sportswriters also took to him as he was articulate and educated and usually gave them good quotes for their stories. He was not the hard-drinking, illiterate, brawler that characterized most players at that time, but just the kind of player that American League founder Ban Johnson wanted - one that would woo ladies and children to the ballparks of the newly founded league. He also had the reputation of being generous to a fault. Although he was known for losing his temper on occasions, he took the customary ribbing from veterans and from hostile fans in good graces. Next to Lajoie he was the most popular player on the team.

After marrying the dark-eyed beauty Lillian, who was three years his senior, they had a son and daughter that Addie adored. He became a home body and was homesick while on the road.

He became pretty adept at telling good stories and also had a good singing voice that led him into joining a barbershop quartet. He also tried the vaudeville circuit in the off-season.

Joss and the team miraculously survived a nasty train wreck en route to a series in St. Louis. None of the players' possessions were ever recovered. Soon afterwards Joss came down with a high fever that required hospitalization. Although no cause was ever found, he may have suffered undetected internal injuries in the crash.

Like other players, Joss needed regular off-season employment and came up with the idea of writing a weekly column for the *Toledo News Bee*. He became the Sunday sports editor,and the page became a major success. Joss' dry sense of humor enhanced his column's appeal, along with providing the reader the "inside dope" known only to ball players. He was confident that he had found his nitch for his post baseball career. He also kept a high profile in Toledo and became one of its stellar citizens.

Joss spent the 1908-09 season studying civil engineering books and even designed an electric scoreboard to help fans keep track of balls and strikes. This "Joss Indicator" was later made part of a larger scoreboard at League Park which also posted the lineups of both teams.[114]

By 1908 he was the premier pitcher in the American League and capped the year by pitching a perfect game against the White Sox and future Hall of Famer Big Ed Walsh, who allowed only four hits and one run while breaking the A.L. record of fifteen strikeouts. In spite of his brilliant year with twenty-four wins, a major league low 1.16 ERA, and five shutouts, his team missed the pennant by half a game. Joss would never get close to a pennant again.

A few fainting spells beginning during the 1908 season did not bode well for Joss. Although he went about his business, he lost his appetite and developed arms problems in 1909. By 1910 his cheeks were sunken, and he had difficulty breathing. He was diagnosed with pleurisy and the doctor missed signs that he could have tuberculosis. By 1911 it was clear that he had tubercular meningitis. The bacteria had traveled to the base of his brain causing severe headaches. There was no cure and no hope. Only two days after his 31st birthday, on April 14, 1911, he was gone.

Joss' funeral was held on a day that Cleveland had a scheduled game with Detroit. Despite orders from American League president Ban Johnson to play the game, all of Joss' teammates insisted on attending the service.[115] This was another indication of the esteem in which he was held by his peers.

Cy Young was especially devastated by Joss' death. "My baseball experience has thrown me with practically every man

---

[114] Alex Semchuck, "Addie Joss," in *Deadball Stars of the American League*. Ed. By David Jones. Potomac Books, 2006, 655f.

[115] *Ibid.*, 656.

in the league for more than twenty years, but I never met a fairer or squarer man than Addie."[116] Young was one of only two non-family members invited to accompany Joss' widow Lillian when they entered the service, and Young wept frequently throughout the service which was the largest Masonic funeral Toledo had ever seen.

Telegrams of condolence arrived from all over the country, including a tender one from none other than Ty Cobb. Lillian asked the famous evangelist and former ball player Billy Sunday to deliver the eulogy at the Masonic Temple where Addie had been a member. A huge crowd of 15,000 gathered in and outside of the Temple. Sunday waxed eloquently stating that Joss "tried hard to strike out death, and it seemed for a time as though he would win. The bases were full. The score was a tie, with two outs. Thousands, yes, millions in a nations' grandstands and bleachers sat breathless watching the conflict. The great twirler stood erect in the box. Death walked to the plate."[117] Sunday went on to declare that Joss, "by his gentlemanly manner, sterling manhood, and unimpeachable honesty was an honor to the profession. He was one of those men who by their character and manhood have helped the game maintain its hold on the American people, from the President in the White House to the newsboy on the streets, from the staid and dignified members of the Supreme Court to the huckster, selling his wares from a wagon."[118] A baseball magazine eulogized him as "a brilliant player, an earnest worker, and a thorough man."[119] Few in attendance would have viewed these statements as being excessive.

---

[116] Reed Browning, *Cy Young: A Baseball Life.* University of Massachusetts Press, 2000, 190.

[117] Cited in Semchuch, 656.

[118] Cited in Longert, 122.

[119] Cait Murphy, *Crazy '08: How a Cast of Cranks, Rogues, Boneheads, and Magnates Created the Greatest Year in Baseball History.* Smithsonian Books, 2007, 292.

It was not unusual in those days for players and others to plan a benefit game for a dead player's family, but Joss' went far beyond the usual. Money poured in with Cobb's $100.00 check the most from any player. The July 24th game between Cleveland and American League All Stars drew over 15,000 people and raised an astounding $13,000, equivalent to a quarter of a million dollars in today's money. The cream of the American League's first decade, including Future Hall of Famers Cobb, Johnson, Speaker, Collins, Baker, and Crawford participated, along with other notables, confirming the fondness and respect in which Joss was held by his peers.

Since Joss didn't complete the ten-year minimum required of entry into the Hall of Fame, the board had to change the rule to allow exceptions for those whose great careers were shortened by death or illness. Thus, in 1978, sixty-seven years after his death, Joss joined the elite players in the Hall.

Hugh Keough of the *Chicago Tribune* wrote a poem in his honor:

He pitched good ball, and what he was beside
He did not say, but showed in gentle acts,
No braggart he, nor puffed with empty pride,
A model for his kind in simple facts.
Just what he was he was and never tried
With vain acclaim to be what he was not.

No strength he bragged nor weakness he denied,
The best he had to give was what you got.
An honest tribute this, from one and all:
He pitched good ball.[120]

---

[120] Cited in Longert, 129.

"Shoeless Joe" Jackson
1888?-1951
Career: 1908-1920

Joseph Jefferson Jackson was an outfielder who played for the Philadelphia A's, Cleveland Indians, and Chicago White Sox.

The mill factories left the North to avoid labor unions and those pesky child labor laws, so Joe probably worked in a Greenville, South Carolina area mill with his father from around age six doing odd jobs before "graduating" to a man's work around age thirteen. Joe never attended a day of school in his life and was illiterate, like many other mill workers.

Professional sports were about the only avenue out of this drudgery, and Joe excelled as a young teen. He could hit the ball harder and throw it farther than anyone else.

He received his nickname on the basis of one game in Anderson, S.C., when he played a game without his new spikes because they blistered his feet. A local sportswriter heard a fan call Joe "a shoeless bastard" after he hit a triple, so the writer began referring to him by that moniker. Joe didn't like the name. He felt it made him look like an ignorant illiterate, and he remained sensitive for the rest of his life to the fact that he could neither read nor write. Joe refused a number of efforts by people to teach him to read, even by the saintly Connie Mack. Joe was not dumb and could have easily learned how to read, so it is somewhat of a mystery as to why he never made the effort to do so. Was it a fear of failure or just pride? At age nineteen he married fifteen-year old Katherine (Kate) Wynn who gladly did all the household paper work. Maybe he was content to let her do all the work.

Joe was relaxed and easy-going, likeable, somewhat naive, and due to his illiteracy, took a lot of abuse from his teammates and foes. It didn't help that Joe used only a knife and his fingers to consume his meals, usually hunching over his plate and engaging in no conversation while he ate. Since a majority of players were from the North they took special delight in harassing a Southerner, especially one with such odd habits. Interestingly, he and fellow Southerner Ty Cobb became good friends partly due to the hostility they experienced from their Northern teammates.

Joe was taunted in every park in which he played. After Joe was traded from Cleveland to Chicago, a heavy-set lady in Cleveland, knowing Joe was illiterate, yelled to Joe: "Hey Joe, how do you spell Mississippi?" After Joe hit a triple, he yelled over to her, "How do you spell triple, fat lady?"[121]

In spite of Connie Mack's best efforts to make Joe feel a part of the Philadelphia A's, Joe never felt at home in the City of Brotherly Love. The merciless teasing and derogatory comments from his teammates didn't help. He also disliked big cities in general, but his first experience in a big city was a disaster. The trade to Cleveland saved his career, as both the team and the city were much more hospitable to him.

---

[121] Bill James, *The New Bill James Historical Baseball Abstract.* Free Press, 2001, 655.

Furthermore, the sportswriters in Cleveland enjoyed the tall tales that Joe could spin about his life and ball-playing days in the South.

Like many players in his day, Joe was superstitious. Biographer Harvey Frommer described how hairpins were one of his fetishes. He seemed to pick up every pin he could find no matter how rusty is was until his pockets were bulging with them. When he went into a slump he would claim that the "charm" had worn off, dispose of them, and start another collection. Another superstition had to do with his wife during home games. When the seventh inning came around, no matter what the score was, Katie would leave the ballpark and go to their apartment to prepare a home-cooked meal. Frommer suggests that this practice was partly nutritional, but also reflected Joe's unwillingness to spend money on eating out.[122]

Joe's other quirks included his never failing practice of keeping a five-gallon jug of corn liquor in his room while on the road, which he used to wash down animal crackers. (Joe, however, was not known to be a heavy drinker.) In addition, Joe would occasionally bring a multicolored parrot on the road which had been taught a few salty dugout phrases.[123]

In spite of these quirks, Jackson pretty much remained the same throughout his career and later life. One significant change was his outward appearance. He had his teeth straightened and cleaned and began wearing very expensive clothes. Possibly his sizeable collection of all types of shoes arose from his self-consciousness over his "Shoeless Joe" label.[124]

Both Cobb and Ruth were amazed at Joe's natural hitting ability. Ruth said that he modeled his swing after Joe, and Cobb marveled that Joe could swing so hard and yet rarely strike out.

---

[122] Harvey Frommer, *Shoeless Joe and Ragtime Baseball*. First Taylor Trade paperback edition, 2017, 35.

[123] *Ibid.*, 66.

[124] *Ibid.*, 62.

Fans and players swore that his line drives sounded different than anyone else's.[125] Cobb assiduously studied the game and all the opposing pitchers, but Joe, though an astute observer of the game, never engaged in anything like a scientific analysis of the game. He was a natural, although he worked hard at learning all aspects of the game. The great pitcher Walter Johnson said Joe was the toughest hitter he ever faced.

Early in his career Joe became the sole support of his mother and eight siblings after his father became ill and died in 1914. This burden, plus his experience of poverty in his early years made him especially vulnerable to the love of money. His fascination with money and nice things would eventually contribute to his downfall.

Joe's marriage to Kate, which was a good one that lasted until his death, was seriously threatened after the 1914 season when Joe found a lucrative way to supplement his baseball income by touring with a vaudeville show featuring "Joe Jackson's Baseball Girls." Kate was left at home for weeks at a time knowing that Joe was with a bunch of beautiful women, and that he was gaining weight and getting out of shape. Kate filed for divorce in 1915, but she and Joe luckily came to an agreement, and she withdrew the suit.

Although Joe and Kate never had children, Joe enjoyed being around kids. Following a game in Chicago, his youthful fans would gather around him, and he would often greet them by name. At times he would stop by a vacant lot and toss balls with kids, using practice balls he had brought with him.

In 1915, Joe was traded to the Chicago White Sox and would spend the rest of his major league career with a team doomed to infamy.

Several things came together to produce the greatest scandal in baseball history. First, by some accounts Charles

---

[125] David Fleitz, "Joe Jackson," in DeadBall Stars of the American League. Ed. By David Jones. Potomac, 2006, 675.

Comiskey was a cheap club owner. His payroll was near the bottom of the league, as was his meal allowance. He forced his players to pay for the cleaning of their uniforms. Virtually all of the Sox players, with the exception of Eddie Collins, felt they were grossly underpaid. Comiskey required the players to play in exhibition games on their off days, which put a lot of money into his coffers, but did not produce a penny for the players. A revealing moment occurred when Comiskey promised his 1917 pennant winning team a bonus if they defeated the Giants in the World Series. After the Sox won the Series, the bonus was a case of champagne! All the owners were cheap, but Comiskey was the worst of that bunch, who made gobs of money and shared little of it with the players.

Second, the failure of the newly formed Federal League, which had removed the hated reserve clause and the ten-day clause (which meant that players were totally owned by the team and not free to go elsewhere unless released or traded, and that a team could cancel a players' contract for any reason on a ten-days' notice) made the players even more bitter. Now the owners had no reason to raise salaries to prevent the players from jumping to the new league.

It is worth noting that Joe was a poor negotiator and was by far the most underpaid star of the game. For example, in 1917 Cobb made $20,000, Speaker $16,000, Johnson $15,000, Collins $14,000, and Joe a paltry $6,000.

Third, the Sox team was seriously divided between the more educated Northern Collins group and the Western and Southern group headed by Chick Gandil.

Fourth, players knew their careers were limited to a few years and depended upon being healthy and productive. Few of them possessed any skills beyond the diamond. Thus, this urgency to grab all the money they could as quickly as they could left them vulnerable to gamblers, who had made inroads into the game over the course of several years. Gambling by players was common and didn't necessarily corrupt the game, but players like the notorious Hal Chase and a few others were widely suspected as having purposely lost games on which they had placed bets.

Apart from gambling and resulting scandal, Jackson's reputation became a bit tarnished when he spent his World War I days in a shipyard instead of fighting overseas. Although many other players took this route, Joe's name somehow became synonymous with "draft dodger" and "shipyard slacker." Joe's reputation with the media of Chicago never recovered from the wartime onslaught of ill will he received from the newspapers.

In addition, the War had the further damaging effect on baseball, in that the racetracks were shut down nationwide and, thus, the gamblers turned their attention to baseball, always seeking inside information from players about injuries, etc., that might impact the outcome of the game. Baseball owners tended to look the other way, wanting to keep the gamblers' activities as unnoticed as possible.

Gandil's promise to Joe that the gamblers would pay him $20,000 proved too much for Joe to resist. Since Joe refused for the rest of his life to talk about the fix, we do not know exactly how he felt about his participation or if he really regretted his actions. It is known that Joe was a distant participant in the fix, as he never attended any of the meetings between the players and the gamblers. Furthermore, Joe only received $5,000. The gamblers double-crossed the players in spite of profiting enormously off of the fix. Only Gandil came away with a pocket full of money ($35,000).

Some have tried to defend Joe in the scandal, pointing out that he had the highest batting average of either team and that he committed no errors. A 1979 book by Donald Gropman, *Say It Ain't So, Joe!* and a more recent one by Kenneth Ratajczak, *The Wrong Man Out*, make a strong case for Jackson's innocence.[126] Walter Johnson, who could find something nice to say about the devil, said that he felt sorry for Joe because, whereas the others were guilty, Joe was only foolish.[127] If only Joe hadn't taken the money, the case for him would be much stronger. Fleitz still contends that the case proving Jackson's knowing participation is too strong to let him off the hook.[128] It's not easy to sort out all the arguments, and no matter which side one takes, there are some questions that cannot be answered to everyone's satisfaction. Baseball experts will surely continue to debate this matter indefinitely.

After his banishment by Commissioner Landis from Major League Baseball, Joe, who expressed no bitterness about the ban, played semi-pro ball (often under a fake name) until he was forty-four years old. Fans in the South still held him in awe and viewed him more as a victim instead of a crook ("suckered into a scheme by fast-talking Yankees"). Sportswriters continued to depict him as an ignorant yokel and/or a scheming crook. By the way, the famous story of the kid who said to Joe as he exited the courthouse "Say it ain't so, Joe" never happened.[129]

After his playing career, Joe, who made good investments as a player, became a successful businessman in the dry-cleaning business, as a restaurant owner, and as a liquor store owner.

Joe's fans in Cleveland certainly hadn't forgotten him. They voted him in as a charter member of the Cleveland Indians Hall of Fame in 1951. Later that year, Joe was invited to appear on Ed Sullivan's "Toast of the Town" television variety show. Joe was

---

[126] Donald Gropman, *Say It Ain't So, Joe!: The True Story of Shoeless Joe Jackson and the 1919 World Series*. Lynx Books, 1970. Kenneth J. Ratajczak, M.D., *The Wrong Man Out*. Author House, 2008.
[127] David L. Fleitz, *Shoeless: The Life and Times of Joe Jackson* McFarland & Co., 2001, 232.
[128] Henry W. Thomas, *Walter Johnson: Baseball's Big Train*. University of Nebraska Press, 1995, 171.
[129] See Fleitz, *Shoeless....*, 277-284.

hesitant to face the scrutiny that would surely come, but finally agreed to appear after much urging by his family and friends. However, ten days before the show was to be aired, a heart attack felled him on December 5, 1951. Kate and Joe's brother David were with him at the time, and it is reported that Joe said to David, "The good Lord will know I'm innocent. Goodbye, good buddy. This is it."[130] Joe was either 62 or 63 years old. Hundreds attended his funeral service, including a handful of major league players and dozens of men who had played with him on the mill and semipro teams. There were so many flowers that the funeral director didn't know what to do with the. He piled them in a tangled heap on top of his grave. This outpouring of affection indicates that he still had many who loved him, whether they believed him innocent or guilty in the Black Sox scandal.

There is no question that Joe was one of the greatest players ever to set foot on the diamond. His record for hits by a rookie lasted ninety years. His lifetime average ranks number three behind Cobb and Hornsby. He probably possessed the best throwing arm of all outfielders in the history of the game. Years ago, F. C. Lane, the editor of *Baseball Magazine*, aptly described Jackson: "Jackson will be known in after-years as the man who might have been the greatest player the game has ever known. To sum up his talents is merely to describe in another way those qualities which should round out the complete the ideal player. In Jackson, nature has combined the greatest natural gifts any one player has ever possessed, but she denied him the heritage of early advantages and that well balanced judgment so essential to the full development of his extraordinary powers."[131]

He would have been a sure Hall of Famer, but his gullibility and his thirst for money ruined what would have been a magnificent career. It is a sad and tragic story.

---

130 Cited in Frommer, 181.
131 Cited in Frommer, 46.

Ross Youngs
1897-1926
Career 1917-1926

Royce Middlebrooks "Ross" Youngs (often incorrectly referred to as Ross Young) was an outfielder for the New York Giants. He was elected to the Hall of Fame in 1972.

Information about the short and tragic life of Ross Youngs is hard to come by. By the time someone wanted to write a biography about him, virtually everyone who had ever known him was dead. Biographer David King[132] expresses his frustration that the countless hours he searched and searched for relevant information yielded precious little information about

---

[132] David King, *Ross Youngs: In Search of a San Antonio Baseball Legend.* History Press, 2013. All of the information in this chapter is culled from this book.

a great ball player whose life was cut short by kidney disease. One has to resort to speculation when it comes to getting at the core of Young's character.

Ross Youngs was born in Shiner, Texas, the third son of Stonewall Jackson Youngs (whose father had been a Confederate colonel), and Henrie Middlebrook Youngs, a local popular singer. The family moved to San Antonio when Ross was ten years old. Shortly after the move the father sold the cattle from the small ranch he managed south of San Antonio, took the proceeds, abandoned the family, and eventually settled in Houston. Ross did what he could to help his mother keep the family fed and clothed.

From an early age it was clear that Youngs was a natural athlete. The rather small (5'6", 140 lbs – later listed as 5'8", 162 lbs in the Hall of Fame magazine) possessed blinding speed and excelled in all sports. Although he had a pleasant personality, he was a fierce competitor on the field. Baseball was his favorite sport, and he was discovered by the New York Giants in 1916 while playing for a minor league team. Showing up at the Giants' spring camp in Marlin, Texas, he quickly became a favorite of manager John McGraw, who loved Youngs's constant hustle. McGraw called him "Pep." Early on his fearless and competitive nature didn't endear him to some of his teammates; but eventually they recognized that Ross was always fighting for the *team*, not for himself. McGraw bragged that the coachable Youngs never disobeyed an order and always responded well to advice without questioning. It didn't hurt that the teetotaler Youngs, unlike many players who were heavy drinkers and often showed up at game time with a hangover, was always in excellent condition and ready to play.

A true outdoorsman Youngs was an avid and talented golfer, spentding his off seasons hunting and fishing.

Ross' good looks and his gentle personality, combined with his fine dancing ability, made it easy for him to attract women. In 1924 he met a Brooklyn girl, Dorothy Peinecke; and after only dating a few months, he and a reluctant Dorothy, tied the knot at St. Paul's Methodist Episcopal Church in Brooklyn. Ross and Dorothy spent the off season with Ross' mother in San Antonio, and for whatever reasons, Dorothy and Henrie didn't get along. Possibly, as biographer King surmises, Henrie, like her husband, also a descendant of Confederate soldiers, didn't like her son marrying a "Yankee." Or, maybe it was the haste of their courtship.[133] At any rate the marriage was over in less than a year. Dorothy filed for divorce during the last months of Ross' life, but Ross died before it ever went to court. Ross' only child, Caroline, was born in Brooklyn, but since Ross maintained his residence in San Antonio, he never saw his daughter. King calls this strange behavior one of the great mysteries of Youngs's life.[134]

During the 1924 season, he developed a case of strep throat and missed several days, but the ever competitive Youngs pushed himself and played anyway. A post season team voyage to cold and damp Europe didn't help. The infection spread to other parts of the body and led to what was referred to as Brights' Disease, causing a severe reduction in kidney function. Despite being weak, Youngs played in ninety-five games in the 1926 season until his body gave out in August.

Things took an ugly turn as Ross filed for divorce late in 1926, alleging "continual nagging" and "harsh and cruel treatment and incompatibility." Furthermore, his mother also had him sign over all his assets to her so that his wife and daughter would have no claim to anything. Although confined to a hospital bed, Youngs remained cheerful and spent his time writing letters to relatives and friends (although his mother penned many of them because the now less than a hundred pound athlete was too weak to hold a pen). His death occurred on October 22, 1927, with the cause of death listed as pyleonephritis

---

[133] King, 110.
[134] King, 121.

(inflammation of the lining of the pelvis and the tissue of the kidney), with myocarditis (heart failure caused by kidney failure) as the secondary cause.

Hundreds, including John McGraw, as well as community leaders from all across South Texas, attended the funeral service at the Porter Loring Chapel, with the eulogy given by Harry Ables, owner of the local Texas League club and the most famous name in San Antonio baseball circles. The service had actually been delayed to enable Dorothy and Caroline to arrive from Brooklyn, but it is not known if they made it.

Two days after the funeral Dorothy sued Henrie for the house and most of Ross's assets. The state court dismissed the case on a technicality and two appeal courts upheld the decision. Thus, Dorothy and Caroline received nothing.

A month before his death, in September of 1927, the Giants honored Youngs with a plaque in centerfield at the Polo Grounds. With John McGraw crying like a baby, Caroline pulled the rope to reveal the plaque. Sometime later the plaque was moved high above the centerfield exit where it remained for thirty years. The Giants left New York for San Francisco in 1958; and it is unknown what happened to the plaque, except that by the time the Mets moved into the Polo Grounds in 1962, the plaque was gone. It has never been found. The wording on the plaque written by sportswriter John Kieran read: "A brave, untrammeled spirit of the diamond, who brought glory to himself and his team by his strong, aggressive, courageous play. He won the admiration of the nation's fans, the love and esteem of his friends and teammates, and the respect of his opponents. He played the game."

The original small stone marker at Youngs' gravesite at Mission Park Cemetery South in San Antonio was replaced with the current marker in 1935 when local leaders and friends raised money with a series of benefit baseball games.

Hugh Casey
1913-1951
Career: 1935-1949

Hugh Casey was a right-handed pitcher, mostly for the Brooklyn Dodgers.

Although there were earlier pitchers who did work as relievers, such as the great Pete Alexander (between starts), Wilcy Moore, and Fred Marberry, Casey redefined the role of relievers. He spent almost his entire career coming in relief late in the ballgame at critical times. He was the first pitcher regularly to be called a "Fireman" as he saved many games for the Dodgers (although the designation "save" would not be officially used until 1969). Casey is also best known to baseball historians, and Dodger fans as the pitcher who threw the famous "pitch that got away" in the 1941 World Series, when Casey struck out Yankee Tommy Heinrich, which would have ended Game 3 except that catcher Mickey Owen failed to catch the pitch. The Yankees rallied and went on to win the game and take the Series.

He was born in the Buckhead section of Atlanta, Georgia, with the blood of the Old South and the Confederacy running through his veins. Ancestors on both sides fought in the War, and his maternal grandfather was age nine when he witnessed Sherman burn Atlanta to the ground. Hugh no doubt heard stories about the conflict during his youth. Like his fellow Georgian Ty Cobb had done earlier, he seemed to refight the War on occasion, although he later jettisoned his racism in a way that Cobb never could. His father was a Fulton County policeman. Hugh loved to hunt and fish in his youth and later became an accomplished hunter.

He was signed by the Dodgers following high school and was mentored in their system by future Hall of Fame manager Wilbert Robinson ("Uncle Robbie" to his players). Robinson became a second father to Hugh. Two years after his major league debut he married Kathleen Thomas, whom he had known in high school.

Sportswriters from early on referred to the burly right-hander as "heavy-set and full-faced." He tended to report to spring training several pounds heavier than the team desired, even to the point where the Dodgers offered financial incentives for him to lose weight. But he never saw his weight as a problem and, in fact, it probably made him appear even more intimidating than he was. He played in an era where it was common to throw beanballs at batters, and Casey became a master at it. For reasons not entirely clear, in his rookie year the *Brooklyn Eagle* newspaper referred to Casey as "sort of (a) twentieth-century Huckleberry Finn," while noting that he was the last pitcher discovered by old Wilbert Robinson.[135]

The Dodgers, under the combative, foul-mouthed, "do anything to win" manager Leo Durocher, were the most hated

---

[135] Cited in Lyle Spatz, *Hugh Casey: The Triumphs and Tragedies of a Brooklyn Dodger.* Roman and Littlefield, 2016, 22. This is the definitive biography of Casey and much of the material in this chapter is culled from this excellent biography.

team in the National League, and Casey fit right in. Casey was the only pitcher that Leo allowed complete freedom on how to pitch in a game, probably because Leo saw in Casey a bit of himself. Plus, "the heavy-gambling Durocher want to keep pitchers Hugh Casey and Kirby Higbe around to ravage at gin rummy."[136]. Casey hated to lose and also had no problem whatsoever in throwing at batters. Leo never had to order Casey to throw at a batter; Casey was only too eager to do it himself when he felt the circumstances demanded it.

An example of Casey's strength and toughness is seen during spring training in 1942, when the Dodgers trained in Havana, Cuba. Writer Ernest Hemingway was living in Havana at the time. He was a big baseball fan. He enjoyed visiting and drinking with several Dodger players, and one evening invited a few gun enthusiasts on the team to his home. Casey was among that bunch. In the course of the evening Hemingway, also a big boxing fan, challenged Casey to a sparing match. Teammate Billy Herman beautifully describes what happened:

> As Hugh was putting his gloves on, Hemingway suddenly hauled off and belted him. He knocked Casey into a bookstand and there goes the tray with all the booze and glasses smashing over the terrazzo flood. Hemingway didn't bother to pick up the tray or anything, and then they were moving back and forth across the broken glass, and you could hear it cracking; and crunching on that terrazzo floor whenever they stepped on it. Then Casey belted him across some furniture, and there was another crash as Hemingway took a lamp and table down with him. . . Hemingway's wife, journalist Martha Gellhorn, came into the

---

[136] Tom Clavin and Danny Peary, *Gil Hodges: The Brooklyn Bums, The Miracle Mets, and the Extraordinary Life of a Baseball Legend.* New American Library, 2012, 58.

room twice during the fight was was unable to get the two combatants to end it. Hemingway was getting sore. He'd no sooner get up and then Hugh would put him down again. Finally he got up this one time, makes a feint with his left had, and kicked Casey in the balls. That's when we figured it had gone far enough. The fighters separated, but it was now late, and the players had to be back at the hotel by midnight. As they were leaving, Hemingway grabbed Casey and said, "You stay here. Spend the night. Tonight we're both drunk. But tomorrow morning we'll wake up, we'll both be sober. Then you and me will have a duel. We'll use swords, pistols, what you want. You pick it."

Herman thought Hemingway was sore that Casey had bested him. "He wanted to kill Casey," he said, but the players left, ending the incident.[137].

In *Bums*, teammate Kirby Higbe added his take on the event by recalling that Hemingway showed up at the ballpark the next day very embarrassed and "apologizing all over the place, almost in tears, He said 'I don't know what got into me.' I knew exactly what got into him. About a quart, that's what."[138]

Fellow Southerner Kirby Higbe was indeed one of Casey's best buddies on the team. Both were heavy drinkers, but Higby was more talkative and friendly, whereas Casey was more of a loner. Instead of going out with the boys after the game, Hugh would usually retire to his room with his big cigars, a Western book or magazine, and his booze. So even though Casey was

---

[137] Cited in Spatz, 109-111. Originally told in Donald Hoenig, *Baseball When the Grass Was Real: Baseball from the Twenties to the Forties, Told by the Men Who Played It*. Coward, McCann & Geoghegan, 1975, 152-155.

[138] *Bums,* 34.

a mean competitor (he once threw at a batter in the on-deck circle) and a hard drinker off the field, he did enjoy playing bridge with some of his teammates.[139].

After his first season with the Dodgers, since most players had to work in the off-season to make ends meet, Casey remained in Brooklyn to sell automobiles, and he became quite good at it. Later he went in business with a friend and opened Casey's Steak and Chop House on Flatbush Avenue. It became a very popular restaurant, and Casey and Kathleen were usually present at night cheerfully welcoming guests. Furthermore, Casey became very involved in civic life in the city, attending numerous local events, such as fund raisers for charities where he signed baseballs and gave speeches. In doing so he became one of the best known and loved citizens of Brooklyn. It didn't hurt that he was the hero of the 1947 World Series. His dedication to civic responsibilities extended beyond Brooklyn as he, like most other players at this time, willingly served in the armed forces. He spent thirty-five months in the Navy when he would have much rather been earning a nice living as a ballplayer.

No discussion of Dodgers players of the 1940s is complete without mention of how they related to Jackie Robinson. This matter is discussed in some detail in the chapter on Dixie Walker. Suffice it to say here that Casey is generally believed to be a part of the group of Southerners, headed allegedly by Walker, that opposed Robinson's joining the team. However that may be, in fact Casey quickly came to see Jackie's value to the club, and even spent hours batting balls to Jackie and thereby helping Robinson adjust to playing first base, which was not Jackie's natural position. In addition, Casey often backed Jackie during rough episodes with opposing players. Most

---

[139] *Bums*, 28.

revealing of all is Jackie's calling Casey "one of the swellest guys I've met." [140]

Although Casey continued to warm up to Jackie and even played bridge with him, there was a painful incident cited by Robinson's biographer, Arnold Ramersad: "At one of those games Casey almost curdled Jack's blood by breezily sharing with him his secret for changing his luck at cards down him in Georgia. 'I used to go out and find me the biggest, blackest nigger woman I could find and rub her teats to change my luck.' Casey then rubbed Jack's hair. In the shocked silence that a followed, Jack swallowed hard, dug down deep, and said nothing."[141]

Jackie's teammate, Roy Campanella, the second black to join the Dodgers, had a tougher time relating to Casey. Neil Lanctot, Campanella's biographer, noted that Casey's racial views were straight out of the old Confederacy and that he was "not keen on taking orders from a black catcher."[142]. Campy adjusted to this by simply letting Casey throw what pitch he wanted to throw.

Casey was indeed a team player, seen also in his willingness to work with young relievers when they joined the Dodgers. He earned the name with them as the "Professor." (I think the only other one to earn that designation in baseball was the other "Casey," the incomparable Casey Stengel). Another black player, Don Bankhead, also spoke highly of Casey, noting that while all the players treated him nicely, Casey, Furillo, and Bobby Bragan were particularly nice to him.[143]. (Note that two of these are Southerners, and that Furillo was initially

---

[140] Cited in Spatz, 179.

[141] Arnold Rampersad, *Jackie Robinson: A Biography.* Alfred A. Knopf, 1997, 178.

[142] Neil Lanactot, *Campy: The Two Lives of Roy Campanella.* Simon and Schuster, 2011, 159f.

[143] Spatz, 223.

against Robinson joining the team. This represents some pretty amazing change of attitudes for that day and age).

Teammate Carl Furillo had things to say about Casey. He said that Casey was basically a nice guy but could be mean and sarcastic, and that he really loved to drink. On the road he would always have at least two quarts of whiskey along with a pocketful of money. "Oh, he went through money like water."[144] Other teammates spoke about Casey's heavy alcohol use. Bill Reddy relates that one night Casey got into a brawl and threw a guy through the plate-glass window of a saloon. But the police didn't arrest him, because he was Hugh Casey.[145] It is also likely that he was not held responsible when one evening he struck and killed an elderly, blind pedestrian.

A major blot on his record, which played a huge role in his mental descent for the rest of his life, was a paternity suit filed by twenty-five year old Hilda Weissman in 1949, claiming that her son Michael was fathered by Casey. It is widely known that many players slept with "groupies" who were available in every major league city, although the press generally ignored this dark side of the game. Casey denied it to his dying day, and Kathleen, although separated from Casey at the time, defended her husband. Former teammate Al Gionfriddo said that Weissman was crazy for ballplayers and that "she screwed just about every ballplayer in the country . . .It could have been anybody's baby." [146]. After three days of court hearings in December, 1950, the three judges took fifteen minutes to unanimously rule in Weissman's favor. Even after the verdict Casey and his wife continued to deny the charges. However, a picture of a grown 6'3" Michael reveals that he is the spitting image of Casey. Interestingly, in 1981, long after Casey's death, his 1947 World Series ring was purchased by the Dodgers from

144 *Bums*, 30.
145 *Bums*, 31.
146 *Bums*, 80. Also cited in Spatz, 254.

a collector and sent to Michael.[147] In addition, the Dodgers also provided a pension for Kathleen.

Sadly, with his restaurant not doing well, his separation from Kathleen, and with the IRS seeking a substantial amount of money for back taxes, Casey was severely depressed. Staying at the Atlantan Hotel, Casey called his close friend, Gordon McNabb, asking him to come to the hotel where "You'll see me but I won't see you." Knowing what that meant, McNabb rushed to the hotel and was outside Casey's room when Casey, doing what his one-time sparing partner, Ernest Hemingway did, fired his 16-gauge shotgun into his neck. Kathleen had talked to Casey earlier that day when Casey told her that he was ready to die, but she could not talk him out of it. Casey's last words to her were, "I am completely innocent of those charges."[148] Although denial and self-deception is common when it comes to sexual activity, it is not impossible, given Casey's heavy alcohol dependence, that he may have been so intoxicated that he honestly couldn't remember the liaison with Weissman.

Although he got his facts jumbled, Casey's buddy Higbe described the suicide this way: "...they tell me he killed hisself over his wife, that he was talking to her on the phone when he took a shotgun, put it to his mouth, and throwed his brains right up to the ceiling. He wuz always crazy about Kay, but they wiz always fighting, and they were separated and he asked her if she was coming back, and she just laughed, and he pulled the trigger."[149]

Funeral services were held on Independence Day at Atlanta's Spring Hill Chapel, and he was buried in Mt. Pavan Baptist Church Cemetery, not far from the sandlots where he played ball. Former teammates Whitlow Wyatt and Dixie Walker

---

[147] Spatz, 260.

[148] In a *New York Daily News* article, cited in Spatz, 264.

[149] *Bums*, 35.

were among the pallbearers. He was inducted into the Georgia Sports Hall of Fame in 1991.

Wall Street Journal writer Joshua Prager provides an apt description of Casey: "Casey threw a curve as hard as he drank, whiskey his preference. He was a loner, had a bad temper and let fly enough beanballs to sate even (Leo) Durocher."[150]

Spatz closes his excellent book with writer Gal Talese's *New York Times* story about the demolition of Ebbets Field in 1960, attended by former players Roy Campanella, Carl Erskine, Ralph Branca, and Otis Miller (who had caught the first game played there in 1913): "When (the crane) reached the 376-foot mark, the workman swung back on this iron ball painted white to resemble a baseball. It came spinning toward the wall, and, after a few shots, there was a hole the size of Hugh Casey." [151]

---

[150]   Joshua Prager, *The Echoing Green: The Untold Story of Bobby Thomson, Ralph Branca and the Shot Heard Around the World.* Vintage Books, 2006, 50.

[151]   Spatz, 272.

Roy Campanella
1921-1993
Career: 1948-1957

Roy Campanella was a catcher for the Brooklyn Dodgers. He was elected to the Hall of Fame in 1969.

Roy was the off-spring of an Italian father and a black mother. His parent's marriage caused an uproar. His father was virtually disowned by his family. Roy was raised in a racially mixed and peaceful neighborhood in Philadelphia. He was a likable kid and was always smiling. He attended the Nazarene Baptist Church regularly and developed the habit of daily Bible reading. He loved baseball from an early age and became a professional player in the Negro League at the unheard age of fifteen (and thus the youngest player in Negro League history). Leaving school after the ninth grade meant that he lacked skills in speaking and writing, but this didn't become a major hindrance, as he had a keen memory, a quick wit, and later became an excellent speaker. He became a close friend with the great Josh Gibson who taught Roy the ins and outs of catching.

At age seventeen he got his girlfriend Bernice Ray pregnant, but she lived with her family and he with his. He spent little time with his wife and daughters for the rest of his life. Attempts to save the marriage failed. Interestingly, even after the divorce Bernice, never remarried and kept his name.

Prior to gaining entry into the major leagues, Roy played in the Cuban winter league and spent two years in the Mexican League (where he became fluent in Spanish). While in the Cuban league he was mentored by future Hall of Famer Monte Irvin, who taught Roy how to get along in a world ruled by white people. Irvin advised Roy to stay out of politics and avoid

controversial issues and confrontational situations.[152] Roy
would follow this advice for the rest of his life. Early on Roy saw
baseball as the only way that he saw out of a life of drudgery
experienced by most blacks. Thus, he never complained about
anything and didn't worry about baseball's reactionary attitude
toward blacks. He was making good money (double the medium
income of his time). He put up with the terrible racial animosity
of the International League without complaint. Black players
weren't allowed to shower with white players, so they had to
wait to shower after the white players were finished. In addition,
death threats were not uncommon during the spring training
trips in the South en route to Brooklyn, including an especially
scary one in Atlanta.[153] On the other hand, it amazed Roy that
he was constantly surrounded by *white* kids who wanted his
autograph.

Signed by the Dodgers and assigned along with Don
Newcombe to Nashua, a Dodgers farm team, his "genuine
friendliness, boyish nature, and wry sense of humor quickly
won over the rest of his Nashua teammates."[154] With few
exceptions he was able to garner the respect and affection
of his teammates for the length of his career. During this time
he met the outgoing and athletic Ruthe Willis of Harlem and
presented her as his wife for three years before they actually
married.

A key ingredient in understanding Roy is his relationship
with Jackie Robinson. After Jackie's hellish first season (1947),
in which he was subjected to unimaginable racist treatment by
opposing teams and fans, he was happy to have another black
player on the team when Roy was called up to the Dodgers in
1948. At last there would be someone who understood, with

---

[152] Neil Lanctot, *Campy: The Two Lives of Roy Campanella.* Simon &
Schuster Paperbaacks, 2011, 98.

[153] Peter Gollenback, *Bums: An Oral History of the Brooklyn Dodgers.*
Contemporary Books, 200, 221f.

[154] Lanctot, 131.

whom Jackie could share his frustrations. Initially the two lived not too far apart in Brooklyn and shared rides to the park, as well as their spending free time together. But these two very different personality types experienced difficulties as each reacted to racism in very different ways. Jackie was intense, argumentative, and combative and was beginning to become more bold as he faced prejudice on and off the field. In his initial season in 1947 Jackie took Branch Rickey's advice to avoid any confrontation. Jackie's good rookie season convinced him that he belonged in the majors, and he shouldn't have to meekly endure what no other player had to put up with. Furthermore, he became more outspoken publicly on civil rights issues. Jackie seemed to take everything personally. By contrast, Roy was constitutionally wired and brought up to ignore any and all slights and hatefulness (e.g., by "nature" and "nurture"), and it disappointed Jackie when Roy refused to tackle racism openly.[155] Although each was careful to not criticize the other in public, their friendship slowly cooled off. Although Roy received the same "welcome" to the Bigs that Jackie did (in his first major league at bat he was plunked in the ribs by Giant reliever Ken Trinkle, and he quickly "discovered that the unprotected skulls of black players were a favorite target for certain major league hurlers who 'let the ball talk for them.'"[156] But Roy was able to push it out of his mind and just play the game. The "fiery"Jackie and the "passive" Roy just dealt with matters differently. It is also possible that Roy felt some measure of jealously toward Jackie in that "Roy seemed somehow to excite no special interest on the part of whites - or blacks - despite his brown skin and great talent. Robinson, on the other hand, was the center of every eye every minute he was on the field."[157] Thus, in contrast to Jackie, Roy was indeed a "conservative" in that

---

[155] See a detailed account of their differences in *Bums*, 226-231.

[156] Lanctot, 160..

[157] Arnold Rampersad, *Jackie Robinson: A Biography.* Alfred Knopf, 1997, 209.

he didn't want to rock the boat that was treating him fairly and generously, even though most black players weren't nearly as fortunate as he was. But, to his credit, he became a mentor to such players as Hank Aaron and John Roseboro and was especially helpful to them in guiding them on how to live away from the ballpark.

In spite of their differences, in their public statements about each other Roy and Jackie generally heaped praise on each other. For example, even though Jackie viewed his 1951 season as his best so far, Roy won the MVP award. But Jackie said that Roy deserved the honor because "he kept us in the pennant race. . .I am convinced that Campanella is the best catcher in baseball today."[158] In later years, Jackie praised Roy for taking a stronger stand against Jim Crow laws.[159]

Except for an incident mentioned later in this chapter, Roy always praised Jackie when speaking publicly.

In another wrinkle, Roy became pals with the Daily News' sportswriter Dick Young, but got caught between Young and his feud with Jackie, leading Roy to later warn his son that "white people will use you to attack other blacks."[160] Roy was also able to navigate the delicate relationship with white pitchers, some of whom didn't like taking orders from a black catcher, and even became more assertive with them while at the same time becoming more animated in his chatter with the hitters in the batter's box.

Although Roy got along well with all the Dodger white players, he was probably closest to Gil Hodges, who was the team unifier. Even when Jackie and Roy grew apart, Hodges refused to take sides and remained close to both of them,

---

[158] *Ibid.*, 242.
[159] *Ibid.*, 399.
[160] Lanctot, 167.

and even served as link between them.[161] Roy's affection for Hodges is seen in Campy's public statement after learning of Hodges' death. Roy noted that Hodges was never booed in any city where he played, that he had the affection and respect of every Dodger player, and that he deserved to be in the Hall of Fame.[162]

His biographer, Neil Lanctot, ably describes Roy's personality: "...what ultimately distinguished Campy from other elite jocks was his personality. Here was a celebrity who was anything but bland and who exuded color from every pore. How many ballplayers looked like a 'dusky whiskerless Santa Claus' but could hit like Joe DiMaggio? How many had such a high, squeaky voice that everyone seems to make fun off, even his own teammates ('Why don't you catch cold and talk like a man?" said Pee Wee Reese). And most important of all, how many superstar athletes were never at a loss for words? Despite his ninth-grade education, Campy's capacity for language was extraordinary."[163] Reese said he was funnier than Bob Hope and could always come up with an expression that would ease tension in the dugout. He seemed to have an inexhaustible supply of witty and wise sayings, with his most famous one being "You have to be a man to be a big league ballplayer...but you have to have a lot of little boy in you too."[164] This friendly teddybear of a man was so prone to drop words of wisdom that sportswriter Frank Graham, Jr., referred to him as a "homey philosopher," something akin to Will Rogers in a catcher's mask.[165]

---

[161] Tom Clavin and Danny Peary, *Gil Hodges: The Brooklyn Bums, The Miracle Mets, and The Extraordinary Life of a Baseball Legend.* New American Library, 2012, 150.

[162] Marino Amoruso, *Gil Hodges: The Quiet Man.* Paul Eriksson, 1991, 140f.

[163] Lanctot, 271.

[164] *Ibid.*, 271.

[165] *Ibid.* 272.

In spite of Roy's generally even temperament and refusal to take the bait to engage in any kind of conflict, one instance with Brave pitcher Lew Burdette indicated that he was keenly aware of the insidious racism directed toward him and which, at times, could boil over. Southerner Burdette had had a running feud with Jackie ever since Jackie stole home against him the year before, and he openly showed disdain against all blacks that were now slowly entering the Major Leagues. Although it was true that Burdette's "bread and butter" was throwing inside, Campy insisted that "my head ain't his bread and butter" following a near brawl in Milwaukee after Burdette called Roy a "black nigger bastard" from the mound. Roy lost his cool and headed toward the mound with bat in hand but was restrained by teammate Carl Furillo and Brave catcher Del Crandall before he reached Burdette. Furthermore, after he purchased a very nice waterfront home on Long Island in 1956 (now that he was the Dodgers' highest paid player), he quickly sensed that as the only black family in the area, he was as unwelcomed as he would have been in the South.

Campy seemed to have simple tastes and interests. He enjoyed his cigars, liked to ride around in his Cadillac, learned to be a sharp dresser, showed great skill in building things, but was in many ways a loner. He possessed a fondness for children, his own as well as others. He also exhibited humbleness when honored. Even though he won three MVP awards, he always insisted that any player on his team - Snider, Furillo, Hodges, Robinson, Reese - could have rightly been given the award. "It was just an honor to play with them."[166]

By 1956 Campy was widely recognized as one of the best (now a three time MVP), but subtle changes were becoming evident. His ego grew and he showed flashes of arrogance. His marriage to Ruthe was in trouble as Roy couldn't resist the many women who were now throwing themselves at him.

---

[166] Clavin & Peary, 132.

By this time he and Jackie now looked at each other with disdain. Except for one off-the-record comment, for the rest of Roy's life he refused to talk about the feud. That one instance occurred when Jackie retired but happened to say to a reporter (also off-the record) that he thought Campy's career was about over. Unwisely, Campy responded to Dick Young's probing and angrily said that Jackie was always shooting his mouth off about something and usually didn't know what he was talking about. In addition, Campy said that Jackie should be leaving baseball with many friends, but instead was leaving with many enemies, and that Jackie was always stirring up trouble in the clubhouse.[167] Roy was horrified to see his statements in the paper, but he should have known better. Dick Young was not to be trusted. He wouldn't make this same mistake again.

Roy's major interest outside of baseball was his 1951 investment in a liquor store in Flushing. He knew he wouldn't play forever, and that he needed to have a basis for a life-long income. Branch Rickey helped Roy set up his new business. It proved to be a good investment for many years. It was a trip from his store to home (although there is evidence he stopped en route to see a lady friend) on January 27, 1958, that would change Campy's life forever. Driving a rental car, he apparently fell asleep at the wheel around 3:30 AM and skidded on a wet road and slammed into a telephone pole. The car flipped upside down, and in the process Roy suffered a broken neck (dislocation of cervicals five and six). Most assuredly, a seat belt, which was only optional on American cars before 1964, would have prevented serious injury. He was five months on a tilt board, which led him into a deep depression as he realized that his paralysis was permanent. For a short time he was suicidal, but the many letters he received, plus his physicians care, brought him to a better place mentally. Specialist Howard Rusk, a pioneer in rehabilitation, helped Roy through this huge

---

[167] Lanctot, 357.

challenge. Observers marveled at Roy's cooperation and dedication to the healing process. He became an inspiration to other patients. The rehab process in the hospital lasted seven months before he could go home. Like most men then, he battled his demons alone and confided in no one, although his children eased his transition from the hospital to home. He refused to blame God.

The Dodgers arranged a benefit for Roy at the Los Angeles Coliseum that was attended by an astounding 93,101 fans, followed by a moving candlelight service. Roy's son, Roy Campanella II, wrote years later that all his family cried when everyone lit matches, making the entire Coliseum look like a huge birthday cake, followed by thunderous applause. "It was a beautiful, touching evening."[168]

Roy was basically an optimistic person, but subsequent surgeries and complications took their toll. He became angry and depressed and began to drink more heavily. His relationship with Ruthe deteriorated rapidly and led to an ugly divorce. Ruthe received the raw end of the financial settlement and she subsequently died at age forty. Roy met Roxie Doles and they were married fifteen months later. She proved to be exactly what Roy needed, as her training as a nurse was put to good use. He adored her two children, and his experience with her and the children seemed to bring him an inner peace. He even had a nice reunion with Jackie.

He was elected to the Hall of Fame in 1969, calling it the greatest day of his life, and gave an excellent five minute speech. He sold his home and liquor store in New York City and moved to Los Angeles where he worked in public relations for the Dodgers. He also attended spring training and worked hard with catchers and was especially beneficial to future Hall of Famer Mike Piazza. He gave frequent interviews and stuck to his script. Roxie was always at his side.

---

[168] Clavin & Peary, 237.

On June 26, 1993, he suffered a heart attack and died before medics arrived. He was cremated and had a private memorial service at Forest Lawn Hollywood Hills.

Following his death some of his teammates were interviewed and heaped praise on their fallen teammate. Pee Wee Reese said that Campy was probably the only ballplayer that no one ever had a bad thing to say about. Carl Erskine said that Roy had a heart full of thanksgiving for all that had happened in his life and who refused to fall into self-pity, Don Zimmer said that Roy was "like a little Santa. Claus. Everybody loved Campy. . .The guy was just one happy, great, lovable baseball person."[169]

---

[169] Lanctot, 428.

Curt Flood
1938-1997
Career: 1956-1971

Curtis Charles Flood was an outfielder who spent most of his career with the St. Louis Cardinals.

Curt Flood would resent being placed in this section for tragic figures. But the fact is that he died relatively young from cancer, and many lamented that he had become a martyr for the sake of other player's welfare. Flood insisted, however, that he was not a martyr: "Don't make my life out to be a Greek tragedy. I live on top of a hill. I'm married to a movie star. I have a wonderful life - though the owners would like me to have a tin cup somewhere."[170] He seemed to have accepted his lot with serenity at the end of his life.

But the fact remains that had he chosen a different path, he may have ended up a wealthy man and a member of the Hall of Fame. Instead, he spent half of his life challenging the reserve clause that had kept all ballplayers at the mercy of their owners. Thus, Flood is known, if at all, for his legal struggles against the owners and not for his successful twelve- year career with the St. Louis Cardinals.

The facts of the case are fairly well known. In 1969, the Cardinals traded Flood to the Philadelphia Phillies. Flood

---

[170] Cited in Brad Snyder, *A Well-Paid Slave.* Viking, 2006, 228.

refused to consent to the trade, but he had no recourse since the owners could do whatever they wanted with their players. Accept a salary offer, accept a trade, or leave the game. Players could not negotiate with another team. Flood called the system no different than slavery, although he admitted that he was a well-paid slave. He refused an offer for around $100,000, a salary at the high end for players then, to play for the Phillies, insisting that the issue wasn't money - it was a fundamental principle for him. He believed that he should have the freedom to play where he wished, and to choose his employer.

Baseball owners, of course, were horrified at this demand. They insisted that baseball would cease to exist if players were free to negotiate with other teams. The majority of sports writers were against Flood, not understanding how anybody could complain about earning $100,000 to play baseball. Many ballplayers, like Ted Williams, Stan Musial, and Bob Feller, spoke strongly against Flood's efforts to bring free agency to baseball. Furthermore, other black ballplayers, like Bob Gibson, Frank Robinson, and Willie Mays, who may have admired Flood for his courage, chose to remain silent in order to protect their own careers. Not surprisingly, Jackie Robinson, Flood's hero, strongly supported Flood and even testified on his behalf. Probably Flood's greatest media ally was Howard Cosell, who went against the media's grain when he openly supported Flood.

Flood's suit against Major League Baseball made its way to the Supreme Court in 1971, and very nearly persuaded a majority to overturn two previous Supreme Court decisions (Federal Baseball Club of Baltimore v. National League in 1922 and Toolson v. New York Yankees in 1953) that had exempted baseball from anti-trust laws. In the end, however, the Court voted 5-3, with one abstention, to deny Flood's case. Brad Snyder in his biography of Flood, uses his legal background to carefully analyze the thinking of every one of the Justices as they weighed the merits of the case.[171]

Even though the ruling went against Flood, it was the beginning of the end of the reserve clause in baseball. The owners, seeing the writing on the wall, agreed to the Player's Union demand to allow a disinterested third party to mediate disputed cases. In 1974 arbitrator Peter Seitz ruled in favor of Jim "Catfish" Hunter's grievance against owner Charlie Finley, thus making Hunter a free agent, but the big case occurred in 1976 when Seitz sided with the Player's Union interpretation of Paragraph 10(a) of the Unified Players Contract. Instead of that paragraph being understood as a lifetime option for owners, which had been the generally accepted view, Seitz accepted the Union's reading that the option was only for one year. This ruling was the result of a grievance filed by pitchers Andy Messersmith and Dave McNally. Seitz declared that Messersmith and McNally were thus free agents.

These two decisions spelled doom for the reserve clause, changing baseball forever. Marvin Miller, head of the Player's Union at that time, insisted that the gains from these two decisions could not have been achieved without Flood's struggle and sacrifice.

Flood's lawsuit took a huge toll on his psyche and on his financial situation. He couldn't deal with the constant media attention, although he generally handled himself well in their presence, articulating carefully his motives and goals in all of this. After a brief and painful comeback attempt with the Washington Senators, one day Flood fled the country for Europe, where he had spent some time previously. Without a regular income, his life came undone and slid down the abyss when he returned to the U.S.

Flood must be admired for his principled stand against what he perceived, and with which many agreed, was an injustice.

---

[171] *Ibid.*, see chapter 16.

He alone possessed the courage to challenge a long-standing aspect of the game.

Flood's moral shortcomings are well known. His baseball life mirrored what another player once said when he confessed that he had spent 75% of his money on women and booze, and the rest he just wasted. Flood was a handsome man who attracted women like flies to honey. In his biography he freely confesses his many infidelities.[172] And, although he drank like most players of his era, the stress of the lawsuit pushed him to a serious alcohol problem that undoubtedly contributed to his death at age 59. After several efforts at treatment, he finally sobered up permanently in 1986. Only then did his life become manageable.

Flood's neglect of his family led to alienation from his children. Fortunately, in the last years of his life he was able to reconcile with them.

An interesting and unusual moral issue centered around Flood's artistic talent. In his early years he displayed some gifts in sketching, although he never developed any skills in painting. He fell into a pattern of sending portrait sketches to a Burbank based painter, Lawrence Williams, who would then turn them into impressive color portraits (the one Flood did of Martin Luther King, Jr. was his most famous one). Flood claimed credit for the paintings. Early on, he didn't think much of this deceptive practice, but when he became well-known for his work, he was too embarrassed to confess the truth. Plus, he needed the money. Flood never publicly owned up to this fraudulent activity, although those close to him knew the truth. It is not a positive aspect of Flood's legacy.

If "all's well that ends well," in a sense Flood ends up O.K. Unlike the sad cases of a Hack Wilson or a Rube Waddell, both of whom died penniless and psychologically damaged,

---

[172] Curt Flood, with Richard Carter, *The Way It Is*. Trident Press, 1971, pp.100-106.

Flood got his act together for nearly the last decade of his life. He married his one-time girl-friend, actress Judy Pace, who proved to be a solid rock for Flood and enabled him to maintain some financial stability while helping heal the rifts with his children. He refused any pity for himself as he battled cancer and showed courage in the face of death. The Player's Association, which had financed his lawsuit but didn't help him when he was destitute, did pay around $400,000 of his health care costs.

By the end of his life, he had won the respect of the players who had kept their distance during the dark days of the legal battles and when Flood was in serious financial and mental straits following the Supreme Court decision. Players who benefitted from his sacrifices by reaping huge financial rewards always thanked him when in his presence. Several players spoke at his memorial service in the First African Methodist Episcopal Church in Los Angeles.

Roger Maris
1934-1985
Career: 1957-1968

Roger Eugene Maris was a right fielder who spent most of his career with the New York Yankees.

Roger Maris could fit into several of our categories, but he is placed in the "Life Isn't Fair" section because of his death at age 51, and because he was largely misunderstood by the public during his career, particularly during the 1961 season when he broke the Babe's single season record of 60 home runs.

The extended family into which Roger was born provides us with a case study in family weirdness. Roger's grandfather and four great uncles were among the two million Slavs who left their homeland prior to World War I to seek their fortunes in America. They eventually settled in Hibbing, Minnesota. As these brothers married into other Slavic families, tensions arose between the several of the families. Roger's father, Rudy Maras

123

(pronounced like "Morris"), was a hot-headed man who was powerfully built and athletic. Rudy married Ann Sturbitz, who was called Connie, a beautiful but angry woman who constantly stirred up trouble with other family members. The family get-togethers were not happy ones. This was not a marriage made in heaven as the couple argued about most everything and clearly couldn't stand each other. Although they finally divorced in 1960, they had been estranged for years.

When Roger was seven the family moved to Grand Forks, North Dakota. Roger's biographers, Tom Clavin and Danny Peary, note that Roger tried to bury his first seven years of life in Hibbing, remaining secretive about what he remembered even though his experiences there would forever influence his life.[173] Interestingly, Roger insisted on listing Fargo, North Dakota, where his family moved to following World War II, as his birthplace. To this day this decision has never set well with the folks in Hibbing who want to claim Roger as their favorite son (along with the city's claim of the other famous native, Bob Dylan). Although the move to Fargo was primarily job related, an important element had to do with getting Connie away from the man with whom she was reportedly having an affair. Unfortunately, the move wouldn't change Connie's life-long penchant of carrying on with other men. Her other character flaws made her an unpopular person in Fargo.[174]

Roger and his older brother, Rudy, Jr., became the star athletes of Fargo, especially in football. Rudy was likely headed

---

[173] Tom Clavin and Dany Peary, *Roger Maris: Baseball's Reluctant Hero.* Somon & Schuster, 2010, 23.

[174] Clavin and Peary mention two instances which illustrate Connie's vicious nature. She told a mother of a boy who had a wandering eye that God was punishing her through her son and that was why he was cockeyed. When Roger was dating his future wife, Pat Carvell, Connie referred to her as "the biggest tramp in Fargo." One wonders if Roger loved his mother or merely tolerated her. Of course, the private Roger never shared his feelings about his mother to anyone. *Ibid.*, 61.

towards a professional career in sports but came down with a mild case of polio following his high school career. Rudy, Sr., to his dying day, told everyone that Rudy, Jr., was the better athlete. Apparently, Roger carried embarrassment and guilt all his life that he, and not his brother, had achieved athletic fame. His father did nothing to alleviate these feelings with his shameless and insensitive putting down of Roger when compared to Rudy, Jr.

Roger was a private person and he never understood why sportswriters constantly probed to fine out all about his youth and his family. To Roger, this was personal information and was off limits to others. Clearly there were enough painful memories in Roger's youth that he didn't want to revisit. Probably Roger's decision to change his name from Maras to Maris in 1954 was another way to distance himself from his past.[175]

Roger spent his high school summers playing baseball in and around Fargo and established quite a reputation. He accepted a scholarship to the University of Oklahoma in 1953 but left the campus after only ten days to return to Fargo to accept an offer from the Cleveland Indians.

Roger's teammates viewed him as a bit of a loner and hard to get to know, but also one who constantly encouraged and complemented them. He was a tough and hard-nosed player, but never looked for a fight. If someone got smart with him, he would warn them that they would suffer the consequences if they persisted. No one can recall anyone taking him up on that challenge.

Like most players who succeed, Roger found a mentor in minor league manager Jo Jo White, who became a father-figure

---

[175] Since the rest of Roger's family changed their name to Maris, some have suggested that it was Connie's doings, due to her hatred of the Maras clan. However, Roger said that the reason for the change was because hecklers on the road would tease him by calling him "Mary-Ass." *Ibid.*, 65.

for Roger. Roger often attributed his success to White's mentoring.

In spite of the fact that Roger was raised in an area where there were almost no black people, he exhibited no racist attitudes and befriended several black players throughout his career. Possibly, being a child of the Depression, he had an understanding and respect for anyone who had struggled to overcome hardships.[176]

Roger and his high school sweetheart, Pat Carvell, were married in St. Anthony's Catholic Church Fargo in October of 1956. Roger had just turned twenty-two, and Pat was twenty-one. Everything points to a solid and happy marriage. In subsequent years all who came in contact with them saw how much they loved each other and how comfortable they were in each other's presence. Judging from comments by their six children, they were attentive and loving parents. As might be expected, Pat didn't get along with Connie.

Roger's major league debut with the Indians was on April 16, 1957. Although he was soon traded to the the Kansas City A's and then to the Yankees, he became good friends with future Indian stars Rocky Colavito and Herb Score.

There was a stubbornness and defiance about Roger that could have derailed his career, but it didn't. He refused assignments, argued with general managers about salary, and took issue with occasional managerial decisions, but his dedication to his team and his giving 100% off-set these traits that were undesirable to management, but were traits that endeared Roger to his teammates.

An event involving the Yankees in 1958, while Roger was with the A's, would end up profoundly affecting his life. On a train trip to Detroit, with the Yankees celebrating their pennant, Yankee pitcher Ryne Duren became inebriated and had a brief scuffle with manager Ralph Houk. Sportswriters in that day and

---

[176] *Ibid.*, 78.

time, who always accompanied the teams on road trips, would have ignored events like this, refusing to publish stories that happened in private. However, Leonard Shecter of the *New York Post* reported the incident to his editor who then turned it into a knock-down, drag-out fight. The story made big news. The other New York dailies were incensed that a competitor had printed an exclusive account of a such a titillating behind-the-scenes story. Now every paper wanted these kinds of stories. This event is often cited as the one that transformed sports journalism.[177] This effort to sensationalize everything would come to full fruition during the 1961 season, when Maris would try to accommodate the writers who would then pummel him in their stories, some of which seemed to have been drawn out of mid-air.

Maris was in many ways a misfit in New York City. His smalltown upbringing left him unprepared for big city life. More importantly, Roger's shy and private nature made for an unpleasant, and sometimes hostile, relationship with New York sportswriters. He could never provide the juicy quote for them to base their story on, or if he did provide one, it was always framed as negative and combative. Roger never felt comfortable with all the probings into his personal feelings and private life. His shyness came across to them as arrogance. When he tried to withdraw from the writers, it often brought even more ridicule from them. While the press often presented Roger in a negative light, his teammates were unanimous in their respect and admiration for him. The Yankee's star player, Mickey Mantle, welcomed Roger to the team and never viewed him as a threat. They became very good friends even though the press often tried to make them appear as bitter enemies.

As noted earlier, 1961 was the year that several sportswriters made it their goal to knock ballplayers off their pedestal. And this couldn't have come at a worse time for Roger. Right when

---

[177] *Ibid.*, 105.

he was challenging the most revered record in baseball, Babe Ruth's 60 home run season, the sportswriters were relentless in pursuing Roger, and succeeded in placing him in the most negative light possible. Usually, Roger tried to answer every question they posed, resulting in hours of questioning after each game. The reporters often pursued him everywhere he went and called him in his room and knocked on his door at all hours. His efforts to kid around with them had the opposite affect that he intended in that what he meant as a gag would be printed as something he meant seriously. He felt betrayed when he was misquoted or misinterpreted. Merely saying hello to a movie star like Ava Gardner would start a rumor that he was seeing her. He couldn't win no matter what he said or did. He couldn't protect himself because it was against his nature to duck questions or to deliver half-truths like most other players did. Sadly, the Yankee front office did nothing to protect him.

Add to this the terrible treatment Roger received from Yankee fans, who booed him incessantly (sometimes after hitting a home run!) because they wanted Mantle to be the one to break the record, and you have the makings of a miserable year for Maris. Hate mail arrived daily. Other fans hounded him for autographs, often interrupting his meals. Possibly no ballplayer ever had to experience such intense pressure from all quarters. There were times when Roger wanted to walk away from it all. Support from all his teammates, especially from his best friend on the team, Bob Cerv, enabled Roger to survive the ordeal. The pressure was so great as he pursued the record that his hair began to fall out. Unlike Mickey and several others who turned to alcohol for relief, Roger found some relief in his chain-smoking.

The press didn't let up on Roger for the 1962 season, calling him the Flop of the Year because he didn't match his 1961 season. And then in 1963 when Roger was caught on camera reacting to a hostile fan by giving him the finger, he became the arch-villain of baseball. Fans believed all the negative things said about him in the papers. By now he was thoroughly disgusted with the press and refused to talk with them. Understandably, the game was no longer fun for Roger and it was evident to all those who knew him.

It was a relief to Roger to be traded to the St. Louis Cardinals in 1967. He was away from the New York sportswriters and was accepted with open arms by Cardinal players and fans. The move also put him into the position of securing a beer distributorship from the Busch family who owned the Cardinal franchise. A change in scenery brought him peace and happiness. To this day Cardinal teammates are effusive in their praise of Maris. Roger received the most fan mail of any Cardinal and most of it was positive. And it didn't hurt that the Cards won the N.L. pennant and World Series on his first year with the team. Icing on the cake was Roger being granted a beer distributorship in Gainesville, Florida.

Following his baseball career, Roger devoted his energies to his successful beer business. His brother Rudy ran the business while Roger used his fame to drum up business and solidify relationships with his clients. Roger enjoyed his work, and especially enjoyed attending the golfing events around the country. He spent a lot of time with his children and deepened his relationship with Mantle.

For years following his years with the Yankees, Roger held a deep grudge against what he had felt was mistreatment by the Yankee organization. He refused to participate in Old Timers' Games at Yankee Stadium. To his credit, Yankee owner George Steinbrenner persisted in his effort to bring Roger back into the good graces of the Yankees. In 1978 Roger finally agreed to appear at Yankee Stadium where he was loudly cheered. Roger and his old teammates were moved by the display of affection he received from the crowd. This day proved to be a pivotal one for Roger as he was able to release his anger against the Yankees and achieve a deeper sense of peace.

Consistently willing to respond to people in need, Maris

participated in many benefit dinners and golf tournaments to help individuals and organizations.

A high point in his retirement was the opening a Roger Maris Museum in Fargo in 1984. Shortly afterwards Roger became seriously ill. What was thought to be a chronic sore throat due to smoking and asthma turned out to be cancer of the lymph nodes. He was told that he was a good candidate for chemotherapy and had an 80% chance of survival. The usual private Maris openly shared his diagnosis and received an outpouring from fans around the country. Upon learning of Maris' illness, Steinbrenner decided to retire Roger's #9 number immediately. On July 21, 1984, Roger's number was retired during an Old Timer's Day at Yankee Stadium. Roger gave a brief but heartfelt speech and was especially pleased that the number of his good friend Elston Howard was also retired on that day.

Upon his return to Florida his condition worsened. But Roger remained hopeful and upbeat and was quoted in *USA Today* with words that would comfort all who knew him: "I have peace of mind. Life has been good to me. I can't complain. Other than a few health problems, I feel good about things, and in the end, that's what counts."[178] He was able to make one final trip to Yankee Stadium where he and Mantle took part in Opening Day ceremonies.

No further pleasure trips were possible as Roger was extremely weak and sick most of the time. No one, however, heard him complain. A trip to an oncologist in Franklin, Tennessee, proved to be too late for someone whose cancer had progressed that far, so he headed to M.D. Anderson in Houston. In spite of several transfusions, Roger succumbed on December 14, 1985, with wife Pat at his bedside. It was on the exact day Elston Howard had died five years earlier, also at the age of 51.

---

[178]   Cited in *Ibid.*, 372.

A few years earlier Roger had bought a cemetery plot in Holy Cross Cemetery in Fargo and was buried there on a bitterly cold day. Mantle, Ford, Richardson, Clete Boyer, and Skowron plus a few other players were present with the overflowing crowd at the service at St. Mary's Cathedral. Bobby Richardson delivered the eulogy. A visibly distraught Mantle sobbed throughout the service.

Six days later a memorial service was held at St. Patrick's Cathedral in New York City with 2,500 attending. Among the very few sports figures ever given such a service at the most famous Catholic Church in America was Babe Ruth.[179] Many ballplayers attended, in addition to former president Richard Nixon and New York mayor Ed Koch. Phil Rizzuto and Roger, Jr. spoke, and Cardinal O'Connor concluded the service by asking the "for one last burst of applause to honor this man."

Sadly, the family's dysfunction continued to exhibit itself. Roger's father had become a bitter man, criticizing Pat, bad-mouthing the Roger Maris golf tournaments, and creating tension at the museum. He was not invited to the New York memorial service. He died in 1982. Connie's presence at events usually heightened the tensions, but Pat and the children were kind to her. Connie died in 2004 at age 90. She and Rudy, Sr., share a joint marker in Riverside Cemetery, a different one from where Roger was buried.

Roger left his family in good shape financially. Brother Rudy, Jr., along with Roger, Jr., continued to run the beer distributorship. An ugly scene emerged when Anheuser-Busch sought to buy out the Marises. When Rudy refused their offer, AB ceased its deliveries, claiming that Maris' company repackaged overage beer. A bitter legal battle ensued but AB finally agreed to pay the Marises $120 million.

Baseball fans will recall that the Maris children were present when Mark McGwire broke Roger's record, hitting #62 in San

---

[179] *Ibid.*, 379.

Francisco during the 1998 season. McGwire hopped into the stands to give the Maris children a hug following the blast. The Maris family came to know and like both McGwire and Sammy Sosa, who also broke Roger's record that year. They were saddened over the revelations regarding the use of performance enhancing drugs by both men.

As is the case with a few other players in this book who haven't been selected to the Hall of Fame, some baseball notables make a case for Roger's inclusion. Maris' stature as a player and as a man has continued to grow as the years pass. Whether or not it will grow enough to convince the Veterans Committee remains to be seen.

PART IV

"WHO ARE THOSE GUYS?"

A gain, some of these men could have been placed in Part II or III in our study, but there is enough complexity and ambiguity in their stories that they merit a somewhat different look. There is a bit of a mystery about them that makes one wonder if we are seeing their true selves, or makes it difficult to comprehend why they turned out like they did. The Nature/Nurture paradox is especially evident in these lives. Did their natural born personalities virtually propel them to do what they did, or was the twig bent by a few, key events? At any rate, they provide an intriguing study.

Hal Chase
1883-1947
Career: 1905-1919

Hal Chase was a first baseman who played most of his career with the New York Highlanders (Yankees)

All of us are acquainted with certain individuals who are smart, gifted, and can charm your socks off. Yet these individuals seem to have no trace of a conscience whatever. What is "right" for them is what gives them what they want. What is "wrong" is what fails to deliver. Often these folks are so bright and charming that they somehow avoid being caught, at least in the short term. They have plausible explanations of what went wrong, and they have convinced themselves that they were not guilty of any wrongdoing. Eventually, however, the chickens came home to roost. In biblical language, "...be sure your sin will find you out." (Numbers 32:23)

Amazingly, although he was implicated in at least a dozen bribery and fixing schemes and had ties to at least thirteen of the eighteen major leaguers either banned or blackmailed, Hal Chase could boast in the end that he beat his accusers in court every time. Indeed, he was never officially banned from the game. Because he was so talented and charming, the baseball establishment often seemed to look the other way.

Raised in frontier California, he later reveled in the amoral and immoral elements of the big city life of the early 20th century. His considerable baseball talents were recognized early on so he threw himself into the one thing that he could do better than most. His tremendous speed was an asset on the basepaths, but it was his agility and grace as a first baseman that won him fame. Most everyone who saw him play concluded he was the best fielding first basemen they ever saw. He was a pretty good hitter, too.

One would be hard pressed to find a worse family man than the handsome Chase. He was married twice, maybe three times, and didn't contest the divorce claims of his exes, Nellie Hofferman and Anna Merion Cherurg, who depicted him as an inveterate carouser who spent most of his substantial baseball earning on things unrelated to his family. He was estranged from his only legitimate son and never met any of his grandchildren, one of whom bore his name. Most likely there were other offspring scattered around that he never knew of and for whom he did not feel responsible.

Amazingly, his son and grandson Hal would insist for years that their famous forbearer was innocent of the charges against him, and sincerely believed that he belonged in the Hall of Fame. In fact, if Chase had been an honest man his accomplishments on the diamond would probably would have landed him in the Hall.

Chase's tenure with the New York Highlanders (later Yankees) exposed him to the dark side of big city life, providing him the place where his worse traits could be honed. It didn't help that the Highlanders owners, Frank Farrell and Big Bill Devery, "personified the dubious morality of early twentieth century New York."[180] Many men of his day succumbed to the temptations inherent in the anonymity of urban life, but they remain unknown because they weren't gifted baseball players or public figures who lives were spent in the limelight.

To Chase baseball, like all else in life, was just a game. He seemed to take nothing seriously, not even the profession that provided him with a comfortable livelihood. By the time he figured out that life was more than a game, it was too late. He had cut short his career, neglected his health and family, and was left a pitiful, shell of a man.

To be sure, most baseball players of his era weren't paragons of virtue. In fact, one writer described the majority of players at that time as crude, ignorant roughnecks, "lower even than circus clowns, itinerant actors, and train robbers."[181] For this reason, the great Christy Mathewson, college educated and honest, stood out and began to change the public's perception of ballplayers. Mathewson and Chase were as different as day and night, and Chase's dishonest play on the diamond forced Mathewson to lose all respect for Chase.

An early example of his irresponsibility and lack of concern for the consequences of his behavior was when he left the Highlanders with a month to play during the 1908 season. This action could have resulted in a five-year suspension and would have ruined his major league career. Fortunately for him, Highlander owner pleaded his case before American League Commissioner Ban Johnson, and Chase was restored with only a small fine. For Chase, getting off easy in a serious situation

---

[180] Martin Kohout, "Hal Chase," in *Deadball Stars of the American League.* Edited by David Jones. Potomac Books, 2006, 712.

[181] Cited in the definitive biography of Chase by Martin Donell Kohout. *Hal Chase: The Defiant Life and Turbulent Times of Baseball's Biggest Crook.* McFarland & Co., 2001, 36.

like this only confirmed to him that he could do whatever he wanted to do and not have to suffer the consequences.

In becoming a very popular player among the fans, Chase's celebrity status went to his head. What little modesty he had displayed as a rookie was soon lost, and he became a selfish prima donna who was not liked by his teammates. He even admitted early on that he didn't play for the love of the game, but only for the money. He wanted to make as much as he could so that he could get into another line of business. This single-minded desire to make as much money as possible would lead any person with no moral compass into shady activities, and this proved to be true for Chase. During his entire career many writers and players suspected that he was on the take, but Chase was so good at what he did that no one could ever produce a case that would stand up in a court of law. He could charm his way out of difficulty.

The most celebrated case against him was when he was playing for the Cincinnati Reds under manager Christy Mathewson in 1918. Mathewson suspended Chase indefinitely for what Mathewson called "indifferent play," a euphemism for throwing games. In spite of affidavits from police, players, and from Mathewson himself, National League president John Heydler was forced to officially clear Chase of the accusations due to a lack of verifiable evidence. Years later Heydler admitted that he thought Chase was guilty but stated that the evidence he was presented with would not have stood up in court. Once again, the charming crook escaped the consequences of his actions, this time with the help of several sportswriters who campaigned on his behalf. Chase did admit to placing small bets on ball games but insisted that he never bet *against* his team. Chase received only a mild rebuke for his "carelessness."

The infamous Black Sox scandal, involving the 1919 World Series between the Chicago White Sox and Cincinnati, opened up the public's eyes to the widespread gambling menace surrounding the game. Not surprisingly, Chase's name emerged several times during the investigation, and not surprisingly, Chase denied involvement. After his major league career Chase admitted that he knew of the fix ahead of time and a grand jury testimony revealed that he made a lot of money betting on the series. Chase denied the money windfall, but as author Martin Kohout observes, "it is hard to imagine anyone, especially Chase, passing up such an opportunity."[182]

Hall of Famer Harry Hooper, whose moral compass functioned well, was dismayed that a few crooks in the game had brought about the Black Sox scandal. He viewed Chick Gandil as the "crook of the bunch," but said that Chase "just wasn't all there," and "just wasn't shooting straight."[183] Hooper could never reconcile Chase's superb baseball skill with his addiction to petty thievery (he took a perverse pride in stealing cigars and other small items), his unsportsmanlike conduct, and his penchant for instigating fights.[184]

Chase did enjoy playing the game and the money he earned from it, so he continued to play in various places in the Southwest following his major league career. But again, he displayed the same aimless and carefree attitude toward life and made no preparations for his future. Alcohol abuse, always a constant presence during his career, became more evident as he aged. Although usually able to find some type of employment, however briefly and undignified, he finally became a "bum," virtually penniless and dependent on others for support. Toward the end of his life, he was described by one writer as "a disheveled, broken figure."[185] His main source of support was his sister Jessie Topham. There is a bit of irony here. Years earlier Chase had purchased a farm for Jessie and her husband Frank and set them up in business. This would

---

[182] *Ibid.*, 239.
[183] Cited in Paul Zingg, *Harry Hooper: An American Baseball Life.* University of Illinois Press, 1993, 189.
[184] *Ibid.*, 189.
[185] Cited in Kohout, 262.

account for Jessie's desire to help, but her husband despised Chase and wouldn't let him in their house, although he did provide him with a little shack on the property that Chase lived in from time to time.

In the last years of his life, it amazed those around him that Chase expressed no bitterness or resentment towards anyone or towards life in general. He maintained his happy-go-lucky attitude to the very end. He confessed that all of his troubles were of his own making and that things would have turned out very different had he made better choices in life. Nevertheless, he would admit only to minor transgressions, steadfastly denying the worst allegations against him. To his credit, he took full responsibility for the failures of his marriages. But remorse was not a part of his makeup.

Various ailments related to his lifestyle and alcohol abuse, landed him in and out of the hospital in the last years of his life. He died at age sixty-four. Kohout doesn't even mention Chase's funeral service. This is not surprising in that Chase was virtually friendless, commanded no respect from anyone, and had alienated his kin. A sad exit indeed.[186]

One baseball historian, Bob Hoie, wrote that "the closest approximation of his personality is Paul Newman in *The Sting* - that is, a rogue, a liar, and a cheat, but ultimately an irresistible character."[187]

Following his death, a surprising outpouring of obituaries extolled his great talent and his great flaws. "Prince Hal" was held up as a great talent that had gone terribly wrong. Some saw him as no more corrupt that many of his peers and even many team owners of his time. Kohout concludes that Chase is such a fascinating character because of the inscrutability of the man. "He comes down to us as a shadowy, grinning figure,

---

[186] Baseball-reference.com says that Casey Stengel and Lefty O'Doul attended Chase's funeral service. See under "Bullpen" on Hal Chase's page.

[187] Cited in Kohout, 5,

and we will never know what really went on behind the pale blue eyes that squint at us through a cloud of cigar smoke."[188] Kohout even thinks that Chase was the most complex, and thus the most compellingly human character in the history of the game. Maybe, but my vote would go to Ty Cobb.

---

[188] *Ibid.*, 278.

Kenesaw Mountain Landis
1866-1944
Commissioner: 1920-1944

Landis received his unusual name from his father, an Indiana physician for the Union forces in the Civil War, who had the misfortune to be wounded at the battle of Kenesaw Mountain near Atlanta, Georgia. As strange as it appears to us today, it was not uncommon for soldiers to name their children after battle sites. (The mountain was spelled both Kenesaw and Kennesaw, and the father chose the former). It is probably appropriate the boy was named after a battle site, since this feisty fellow would be enveloped by conflict for most of his adult life. Indeed, he seemed to enjoy conflict.

Although both sides of Kenesaw's family sprang from deeply religious roots - his father came from a line of Swiss Mennonites and his mother descended from a line of clergy - Kenesaw would eventually establish a reputation as a religious skeptic, and it is possible that he was an atheist. Like many are wont to do, he was comfortable with much of the ethics that flowed from the Christian faith, but never found a home in a church. David Pietrusza, the author of the definitive work on Judge Landis, notes that "While (Landis) failed to inherit his ancestors' religious zeal, Kenesaw did inherit their I-am-speaking-from-Holy-Writ mein."[189]

From his father the Judge also inherited a combative nature and, combined with sibling rivalry with four aggressive and successful brothers, enabled this small man (5'6", 130 lbs.) to intimidate virtually everyone he met. Kenesaw was fearless and strong-willed, and these traits were forever on display as a judge and as baseball commissioner. Even within his ambitious family he stood tall. His siblings referred to him as "Squire," due to his lordly manner, and that moniker stuck with him throughout his entire life.

After dabbling in several ventures (store clerk, errand boy, entrepreneur, short-hand reporter), while serving in the office of his mentor Charles Griffin, Secretary of State, he took advantage of a state law that enabled him to secure admission to the bar, although he had no preparation or qualifications. The only qualification was that one be twenty-one and have a good moral character.

He later enrolled in Cincinnati's YMCA Law School, but since he was neither a high school or college graduate, he was viewed as a rube and an outcast. Seemingly this sense of ostracism never left him, and it made him work even harder. He completed his senior year at Chicago's Union Law School.

Another mentor, Walter Gresham, was appointed Secretary of State by President Grover Cleveland, and took Landis along to serve on his staff. It was here that Landis learned how to handle the press, a skill that would serve him well for the rest of his life. Landis ruffled some feathers in that office with his outspokenness and with his refusal to display the same

---

[189] David Pietrusza, Judge and Jury: *The Life and Times of Judge Kenesaw Mountain Landis.* Diamond Communications, 1998, 4. Most of the material in this chapter is gleaned from this thorough work.

ostentatiousness of some of his colleagues. His populist approach to people endeared him both to Secretary Gresham and to the common man. His good common sense and his savvy discretion made him a force to be reckoned with.

Following his service in Washington, Landis returned to Chicago to practice law. He soon married Winifred Reed. Two of their three children would make it to adulthood, with son Reed Gresham Landis becoming the apple of Landis' eye.

Landis' connection with the progressive wing of the Republican Party landed him a judgeship when a new District Court was created in 1905, following the election of Teddy Roosevelt. In this imposing courtroom, with mural of King John of Runnymede on one wall and Moses on Mt. Sinai on the other, Judge Landis would hold court for the next fifteen years. Landis refused to wear a robe, but that didn't keep him from many theatrical outbursts through those years. He developed a reputation as one who could come down hard on corporations, but always everyone sensed that he was fair and honest in his judgments.

At a time when the federal judiciary could be counted on to rule in favor of business, it was rather startling when Landis ruled against Rockefeller's Standard Oil in an anti-trust case, imposing the largest fine ever in an American court. The decision, which would be later overturned by the Seventh Circuit Court of Appeals (in which the court severely criticized Landis for his "arbitrary" decision and for his abuse of "judicial discretion")[190], elevated Landis to near cult status. Common people felt they had an honest judge who would look out for the common good. There even emerged a modest Landis-for-president movement. In spite of the court's reversal, Landis was somewhat vindicated when another court dissolved Standard Oil.

Even though Landis was developing a reputation as a

---

[190] See Pietrusza, chapters 5 and 6 for a detailed account of this case.

no-nonsense judge who might dispense the maximum penalty on defendants, there was another side to the Judge that is vividly illustrated in a case involving a pimp being tried in his court. When the Judge asked the defendant why he was not wearing an overcoat on a bitterly cold day, the man responded that he had lost his coat. Landis then proceeded to give the man his coat. When the workday ended and Landis was walking home (which he usually did) without an overcoat, someone asked him about the absence of his overcoat. Landis responded that he had "used it to light a fire to keep warm inside of me the spirit of charity that life in a great city like Chicago tends to freeze."[191] So much for the image of an unfeeling grouch.

Landis also displayed uncommon courage when he launched an investigation of organized crime in Chicago (which had been described by one observer as "the only completely corrupt city in America"). Threatening phone calls to Landis' house did not deter him. Even though his effort was unsuccessful, it further cemented his reputation as a judge people could believe in.

World War I brought out the deeply patriotic side of Landis (enhanced surely by the fact that his son Reed was engaging in very dangerous duties in Europe). Landis seemed to go out of his way to suppress dissenters, earning him the title "the scourge of the disloyal." His statements to defendants were often brutal.

The judge also took up the cause of Prohibition and spoke out regularly about the evils of alcohol. He fought the repeal movement, which he should have known was a losing proposition.

Landis' image on the bench is aptly described by one writer as "Small on the huge bench sits a wasted man with untidy white hair, an emaciated face in which two burning eyes are

---

[191] *Ibid.*, 95.

set like jewels, parchment-like skin split by a crack for a mouth; the face of Andrew Jackson three years dead."[192]

The turning point in the Judge's life, of course, occurred when he was offered the job of baseball commissioner in 1920. Baseball was still reeling from the infamous Black Sox scandal which threatened to destroy the game. Baseball owners realized that a strong commissioner was needed to deal harshly with the gambling menace that threatened to overwhelm baseball and help restore integrity to the game. Landis would not accept the position unless he was given dictator-like powers. The owners were desperate enough to grant him unprecedented power along with a huge $50,000 annual salary. The Judge was not bashful about exercising his power.

As all baseball fans know, even though a jury acquitted the eight White Sox players, Landis nevertheless banned all of them from baseball forever. He showed no mercy to Buck Weaver who many thought should be allowed to play. Although Weaver accepted no money and played well during the series, the Judge ruled that since Weaver knew about the scheme and didn't report it, he was just as guilty as those who took the money. One can make the case that the Judge's decision, especially the one related to Weaver, pretty much ran the gambling crowd away from baseball. Now players are very aware that refusal to participate in a fix was not enough. If he knew something was brewing, he had to notify the commissioner's office or face possible banishment from the game. Not many players were willing to take the risk of remaining silent with the certainty of such punishment.

Authors Lyle Spatz and Steve Steinberg in their book, *1921*, deal at length with Landis' verdict regarding the eight players. They admit that focusing on these eight was scapegoating, but Landis understood, quoting another writer, that moralistic posturing, particularly about gambling, brings greater rewards

---

[192] Cited in Pietrusza, 122.

than actually trying to do something about the vice in question. By focusing on the players, Landis deflected attention from the owners and their repeated failures to confront gambling in baseball. Landis was thus rehabilitating the game by narrowing the focus, simplifying events, and making examples of a few attractive suspects. While his actions, and those of the owners, were indefensible, it was at least understandable. Landis' great wisdom was in understanding that any attempt to investigate all the gambling and fixing of the past would not only be impossible from a purely administrative standpoint, but would open up a can of worms that would eat away at baseball for the next decade. Had Landis gone after every dirty player and every thrown game, the very fabric of baseball might have unraveled.[193] What he did in banning the eight forever from baseball was a public relations masterstroke. Charles Alexander agrees: "If somewhat self-contradictory, frequently despotic and nearly always arrogant and bombastic, Landis was also probably indispensable under the circumstances."[194]

Never one to avoid controversy, Landis insisted on keeping his judgeship even after he took the commissioner's job. It wasn't a "double dip" in that Landis used his $7,500 federal salary to reduce his commissioner's salary by the same amount, but criticism was persistent that he couldn't do justice to both responsibilities. It is likely that Landis' persistent nemesis, Ban Johnson, who had virtually ruled baseball for two decades and resented Landis' extraordinary powers, was the main person behind the negative campaign against Landis. Landis fought against this effort, but as the criticism slowly died down, Landis went ahead and gave up his bench anyway.

In spite of the Judge's keen political interests and in spite of regular calls for him to run for some office (mayor of Chicago,

[193] Lyle Spatz and Steve Steinberg, *1921: The Yankees, the Giants, and the Battle for Baseball Supremacy in New York.* University of Nebraska Press, 2010, 13, 16.
[194] Cited in Spatz and Steinberg, 209.

governor of Illinois, even president), Landis never really seriously considered those options, although he seemed to enjoy the attention he received. He clearly liked to have his ego stroked.

As Landis aged, he left his more progressive stance and became more conservative. He also took up the plight of war veterans with great vigor, supporting the veterans' call for a bonus (although Landis hated that word and insisted that paying the veterans what they had deserved in the first place was a moral and national obligation and not a "bonus"). He delivered stem-winder speeches in a number of places in support of this cause.

By the end of the 1920's Landis had stopped speaking out on non-baseball issues. Both Prohibition and the "bonus" issue were now dead causes and he had burned up a lot of energy that he no longer had. From here on out his total focus was on baseball.

A tense moment occurred when the much-loved Babe Ruth organized post-season exhibition games ("barnstorming") in 1921 in direct violation of league rules. There was considerable risk in the Judge taking on the most beloved player in the game, but, somewhat surprisingly, the public took the Judge's side, even though many viewed the rule as unfair. After the Judge exiled the Babe for six weeks, Ruth eventually backed away and avoided a nastier confrontation. The Judge had stared down the national idol, all the while knowing that he had to have public opinion on his side. He had it. As it turned out, later the owners amended the rule.

During Landis' long tenure there was no lack of difficult situations that made him call on his experience and wisdom to find an acceptable solution. He generally succeeded in reaching a conclusion that seemed fair and was at least tolerable to those on the losing end. His ruling on the Tris Speaker-Ty Cobb alleged gambling on a game was one of the biggest. Landis didn't ban these two superstars from the game, but it has to be noted that both men never managed in the big leagues again. He had apparently worked out something behind the scenes that would be both fair regarding the charges and not detrimental to the game.

Whatever else Landis was concerned about, the issue of gambling was clearly at the top of his list. He was bound and determined that another Black Sox scandal never happen again in baseball. In his view if there was no gambling there could be no bribery of players. He remained totally inflexible about the issue. He couldn't forbid players from betting on other sports, but he certainly tried. The great Rogers Hornsby wagered large sums of money on horse racing and Landis hated it, and eventually blacklisted Hornsby from the majors following Hornsby's dismissal by the Browns. Hornsby remained unrepentant, insisting that what he did was legal and in no way affected his life in baseball. Landis didn't budge and Hornsby never was able to secure a coaching or managing job in the majors. Landis had similar feuds with future Hall of Famers Leo Durocher and Gabby Hartnett regarding their associations with known mobsters. To Landis the very appearance of impropriety was enough to demand that ballplayers should have nothing whatsoever to do with anyone remotely associated with gambling.

Landis deserves credit here. He was keenly aware that the public was still wary about the integrity of the game following the Black Sox scandal, and that he had to go to an extreme to protect the game. Most knowledgeable baseball experts agree that without Landis' forceful, dictatorial actions, the game would not have recovered from the scandal. The Judge wasn't afraid to take on anything and everyone that might threaten the game. In so doing it is safe to say that even the club owners were terrified by him throughout his tenure. His affection was for the players, whether great or average, and he could not have cared less what the owners thought of him. On several occasions he threatened to resign when the owners bucked him; they always backed away.

Landis was even willing to take on the powerful Branch Rickey on what Landis perceived to be unethical actions. Landis thought Rickey was sanctimonious and moralistic and often referred to him a "that hypocritical preacher" and "that Protestant bastard who's always masquerading with a minister's robe."[195] Landis later regretted that he hadn't barred Rickey from the game due to his shady dealings with minor league clubs and his ability to hide good players from other clubs.

Outside of his job, Landis loved to play golf (although he was horrible at it), fish, talk politics, and read. He and his wife Winifred were devoted to each other. Landis was fiercely loyal to his family. As one observer put it, "There are only three things Landis cares about. They are fishing, baseball, and his son Reed."[196] He rarely drank alcohol, but he smoked heavily. He referred to God enough in his speeches to discount the view of some that he was an atheist, but he had nothing to do with organized religion and was generally critical of it.

Author David Pietrusza devotes a lengthy chapter to a controversial issue surrounding Landis' tenure as commissioner - the race issue. Some critics have sought to place the sole or at least the primary blame on Landis for preventing the integration of baseball, noting that it was only three years after Landis died that baseball was finally integrated. Pietrusza finds little documentation that would either condemn or defend Landis.

There is no record of the Judge engaging in any prejudicial actions in his personal life. In fact, he regarded his two longtime black domestics, Leonard and Elsie Edwards, as friends and took care of them financially in their old age. Like virtually all those associated with the game in his day, Landis resisted integration, but his primary motivation was always to protect major league baseball. It is known that he discouraged play between white players and Negro League players because the Negro

---

[195] Cited in Piertusza, 361.
[196] Cited in Piertusza, 109.

teams generally outplayed and beat the white teams, causing embarrassment to major league baseball. Furthermore, those interracial games were often played before larger than normal crowds, which brought further embarrassment to the league.

In addition to the embarrassment factor, Landis worried about possible race riots in interracial contests (a genuine fear in his era because of the history of race riots in northern cities during his lifetime), and he also didn't like the association that many black team owners had with known gamblers. Also, there was the threat of bidding wars to secure the best Negro players, and this could have unleashed forces that would have challenged the entire pay system in the game.

Pietrusza also examines Bill Veeck's charge that Landis prevented integration and concludes that the evidence doesn't back up Veeck's charge. Pietrusza rightly concludes that it is patently unfair to make Landis the major roadblock to integration, but Landis also showed no courageous leadership to correct a clear injustice that permeated the game. The Judge seemed to be no better or worse than virtually everyone else in leadership positions in his era regarding racial justice. Although Landis was nurtured in the more progressive wing of the Republican party, which might have prompted him to be more open to needed changes, he clearly wanted to "conserve" the national pastime that had prospered so well under its current arrangements.

Although not well known about the Judge, he was ahead of his time when it came to the reserve clause. He gave a sympathetic ear to players who felt used and helpless in the farm system and in the system in place with reference to their owners. In a few instances he ruled in favor of players and against the owners.[197]

One writer in Landis' day says that Landis would have been a great tragedian. "He has a natural sense of the dramatic, a

---

[197] See the discussion in Brad Synder, *A Well-Paid Slave: Curt Flood's Fight for Free Agency in Professional Sports.* Viking Press, 2006, 99f.

splendid sense of humor, a severity that has been call brutal, and a sense of right and justice and morality splendidly and consistently in keeping with the conventions of the time."[198]

Pietrusza nicely summarizes the Judge's legacy:

Restoring and maintaining the public's faith in baseball was what the owners had hired their new commissioner to do when they crowded into the back of his courtroom in December 1920. It was not easy task. The Squire may have been arbitrary, capricious, old-fashioned, vindictive, and more than occasionally profane, but no one could deny Kenesaw Mountain Landis had accomplished what he had been hired to do.[199] Indeed, today we can take it for granted that baseball is honest, and we take it for granted because of Landis.

Landis' health deteriorated quickly in 1944 as he was hospitalized for various ailments. He was eager to leave the hospital on Election Day, November 7, just so he could vote against Franklin Roosevelt (whom he despised), but he was unable to do so. He suffered an apparent heart attack and died in the early morning of November 25th. Following his wishes, he was immediately cremated and no services were held. His ashes were later interred, and a modest headstone erected. Two weeks later a special committee named him to the Hall of Fame.

[198]   Cited in Piertusza, 143.
[199]   *Ibid.*, 452.

Paul Richards
1908-1986
Career: Player: 1932-1946; Mgr.: 1951-1976

Like many successful managers, Paul Richards was not an outstanding player. He was a pretty good player, but had he not managed he would barely have been mentioned, if at all, in the history of baseball. And, like many other successful managers, he had no need to be liked. He wanted respect from his players but lost not a minute of sleep over a players' dislike, even hatred, of him.

Richards was born and raised in Waxahachie, Texas, in a house that stands to this day. The building today houses The Plantation Restaurant, and not only serves excellent food but has a notebook where people write about their encounters with ghosts in the house. None of the accounts fit Richards' description. Nor have there been any sightings of his ghost on the golf course there where he spent countless hours throughout his adult life and where he, fittingly, breathed his last breath. In his youth there was a strong bond with his father, but he pretty much kept his distance from his difficult mother.

He was a quiet thinker who often seemed to be in a world of his own. It was because he was always thinking ahead during a game. He was not given to affirming his players, but with few exceptions he would only criticize them, which he often did, in private. He liked to brag that one of his players said that he "had the personality of a doll . . .a crocodoll." He enjoyed playing the role of a tough Texan. A good friend said that Richards awoke every morning, looked in the mirror and said, "I'm Paul Richards, and I'm tough." Not surprisingly, for some players this tough disciplinarian was either the best manager they ever played for or the worst one.

Brooks Robinson said that Richards was the best man in baseball he had ever met. "I mean, he was like a God to me. He just knew more about the game than anyone I've ever met. . . (He) was a disciplinarian. It was my way or the highway. . . He taught me things about the game that I never even thought about. . .he just knew every phase of the game."[200]

Pitcher Jim Brosnan, who kept a diary during the 1959 season, published originally in 1960 as *The Long Season*, heaps praise on Richards. In his April 5th entry, during the Grapefruit League in Florida, he said that "Paul Richards should get an Academy Award for best direction in a dramatic presentation. Any manager who can win fifty games with that crew is an awesome genius...If he's not the best, then there isn't any best. . . just a few better-than-average managers."[201]

---

[200] Fay Vincent, *We Would Have Played for Nothing: Baseball Stars of the 1950s and 1960s Talk About the Game They Loved.* Simon & Schuster, 2008, 237-241.

[201] Jim Brosnan, *The Long Season.* Ivan R. Dee, 2002, 55.

Richards was a man of conflict from the outset of his sixty-year career in baseball. He would end up being thrown out of more games than any other manager of his time. Although he rarely used profanity elsewhere, he used language in his arguments with umpires that would embarrass a sailor. One umpire said he had the foulest mouth in the major leagues. Interestingly, Richards seem to display his hot temper only towards umpires, and rarely directed his anger toward a player.

Early on in his managerial career he was referred to as "The Wizard of Waxahachie," for his innovative and often daring strategy. He saw himself as a teacher of men, spending hours coaching players in the fundamentals of the game. He believed that it was impossible to practice too much. He wasn't quite the hard driver that John McGraw was, but he was a close second. He worked his players hard to get them in playing condition. He refused to get close to any of his players because he knew it might skew his decision as to whether or not they were a benefit to the team as a whole. Thus he came across as cold and aloof.

There was also a devious streak in him. His driving desire to win caused him to cheat his friends on the golf course. Even his daughter called him a con artist. He could fool players, owners, sportswriters, friends, and golf buddies. Since there wasn't usually a lot of money involved here, it is puzzling what drove him to engage in this kind of behavior. In spite of commanding a decent salary, he didn't deny that he padded his expense accounts, apparently believing that it was standard procedure for managers to do this. He also violated rules by trying to hide players from other teams who might be interested in them. He also was guilty of paying bonuses under the table in order to avoid the bonus limit which demanded that players receiving over a certain amount were to be placed on the major league team and not sent to the minors. To be sure, other teams were accused of this subterfuge as well. It was not uncommon to hide a bonus by hiring a player's father as a scout. For engaging in things like this, one baseball executive called him a man of questionable character.

He was a good student and an avid reader, although he never finished high school. He had a particular interest in American history, with Lincoln being his favorite figure. He also studied military figures, especially the Nazi general Erwin Rommel, for insights into leadership. It might come as a surprise that for years he taught a boy's Sunday School class in the First Baptist Church of Waxahachie. He always carried a Bible with him on the road.

Like Rogers Hornsby, he was totally dedicated to the game of baseball. While Richards' outside passion was golf, and Hornsby's was gambling, both of these men lived and breathed baseball twelve months a year. Both were sore losers and felt that even when they won it could have been done more artistically or quicker.

Since he was a sleepwalker, he earned the nickname "Sleepy" in high school, a name he didn't like. He also didn't like the nickname "Tex," given to him by his teammates at the beginning of his playing career.

In 1932 he married hometown girl Margie Marie McDonald, a school beauty. They would spend 50 years together before her death in 1982. She would follow Paul wherever baseball took him without complaining. There is no indication that he ever cheated on her, unlike many ballplayers in his day. When he was on the road, he would call home and engage in long talks with her. In fact, his daughter Paula was rather stunned when she realized as her mother was dying that so much of her parents' decision making took place on the phone. Paula discovered this when she witnessed a phone conversation after Margie was told of her terminal condition. Her parents had a long talk about what would happen next, but likely couldn't have carried on this conversation face-to-face. This observation coincides with what Hank Aaron said about Richards, that he would look out the window during meetings with Hank and never look at him. It was like Aaron wasn't even in the room.[202] It seems that Richards hid his shyness behind a persona of arrogance and non-caring aloofness.

Richards helped his daughter Paula become a horse breeder and promoted an independence in her that was ahead of the times. His only other child, Lou Redith, died from a heart ailment at age five.

As a player he was a mediocre hitter and fielder but managed to spend a few years in the majors as a catcher because he was so good at handling pitchers. He was ambidextrous and even pitched both left and right-handed in a few minor league games. His main claim to fame was that he became the personal catcher for future Hall-of-Famer Carl Hubbell. Hubbell's famous screwball convinced Richards that every pitcher must master a change-up. Later, his ability to spot a pitcher in-the-rough, his patient development of young pitchers, and his skill in rehabilitating veteran pitchers that everyone else had given up on, was probably his greatest gift. He seemed to instinctively know how to motivate each pitcher individually so that they would gain confidence in themselves. Hall-of-Famer Hal Newhouser attributed his success to Richards. His emphasis on pitching, defense, and aggressive base running would be hallmarks of his teams. He also stressed teamwork and believed that games were not won but lost. The "secret" of the game was not to beat yourself.

His innovations included platooning players (although it was called alternating then, even going so far as to move a pitcher to another position and bringing him back to the mound after a reliever had faced one or two batters), instituting a pitch count, especially for young pitchers ("a tired pitcher is a badly handicapped pitcher"), and his most famous one - the development of the huge mitt to catch knuckleball pitchers. He

---

[202] Hank Aaron with Lonnie Wheeler, *I Had a Hammer: The Hank Aaron Story*. HarperCollins, 1991, 187.

also developed what would later be called On Base Percentage (OBP), apparently the first to keep track of not just one's batting average, but how often they reached base for any reason.

His characteristic stubbornness at times proved to a moral strength. For an exhibition game in Birmingham he was asked to not play his black players, to which Richards responded, "I'm sorry, but that question of racial segregation was settled more than 2,000 years ago on Mount Calvary . . .Christ Jesus died for us all."[203] He believed that his racial attitudes were enlightened. On the other hand, several black players who played for Richards felt that he didn't like blacks in general and never said anything good about them. One black player, Joe Durham, went so far as to call him a "hypocritical racial son of a bitch."[204]

Richards tended to build a "good ole boy" network that followed him around to the various teams he managed. Lum Harris, Jim Busby, Clint Courtney, and a few others were brought on as coaches or scouts whenever Richards moved to another team. He was probably closest to Lum Harris, but it is puzzling to learn that after both of them were fired from the Atlanta Braves in 1972 they never spoke to each other again.[205] Future Hall of Famer George Kell was one of the few of his players with whom he built a relationship.[206] They were golf buddies and Kell was one of the very few people who could tease or needle Richards. His relationship with the press was at best testy.

---

[203] Warren Corbett, *The Wizard of Waxahachie: Paul Richards the End of Baseball as We Knew It.* Southern Methodist University Press, 2009, 184. Most of the information about Richards in this essay is found in this definitive biography.

[204] *Ibid.*, 183.

[205] *Ibid.*, 342. Harris related to the author that he had written Richards one of the sincerest letters he had ever written, but Richards never even replied.

[206] George Kell with Dan Ewald, *Hello Everybody, I'm George Kell.* Sports Publishing, 1998, 96f.

One writer described him as "a cold and hard man. Yet when he chooses to relax the imperious reserve that cloaks him he can charm a ball player right out of his spikes, and the loyalty he elicits from the few who knew him well is a rare and most unusual thing."[207] Another writer observed that "There was a look fathers used to give their kids, where you just backed off when you saw it. Richards had that."[208]

Dogged attention to details was his hallmark. He fined any of his coaches who couldn't tell him which way the wind was blowing. He believed that games were won by being alert to the smallest detail and drilling his players to be that way. He felt that the hit and run and the squeeze bunt were overrated. He favored the run and hit instead. He agreed with Connie Mack that pitching was 75% of baseball. The intentional walk was a dangerous gamble, so he rarely employed it. His teams bunted more than most but later changed his mind and felt that the sacrifice bunt was the most overrated tactic in the game.

He was not an inspirational leader and his approach to the game was analytical and unemotional. He believed that restraint was absolutely necessary for a manager. Thus, he often seemed aloof.

Jim Russo, a longtime Oriole scout, said that "Richards was one of the few people I ever meet in baseball who had absolutely no sense of humor. And he wanted total control of the team. He even complained about the vendors at Memorial Stadium. He didn't want them bothering the pitchers in the bullpen or getting too close to the dugout during the games."

As noted earlier, Richard's only other passion besides baseball was golf and he devoted a huge amount of time playing it. He almost always bet on his games and probably won a lot of money because he would cheat at times (tee up a ball in the rough), needle his opponents and find other ways to

---

[207] Cited in Corbet, 238.
[208] Cited in *Corbet*, 249.

throw off their concentration. He won a few tournaments and even established a tournament in his hometown.

He was a vigorous opponent of the player's union, believing it to be a great threat to the game and stating that the dropping of the reserve clause "would end baseball as we know it," comparing players getting rid of the reserve clause to "the Pope burning down the Vatican."[209] He was a company man all the way. He was right to see that lifting the reserve clause would indeed cause players to change teams regularly, thus making it hard to fans to identify with a team that was constantly changing personnel.

Following the death of his wife in 1983, Richards survived colon cancer and underwent heart surgery. Sportswriter Blackie Sherrod said that though Richards was reduced to skin and bones, "he could go through a platter of baby back ribs like a liberated POW."[210]

He spent his last years with his baseball friends, but it is revealing how one friend, Eddie Robinson, described him: "He never exhibited how he felt really close to you, you know, but you just knew he did. Never threw his arm around you, like some people will grab you and all that shit. That wasn't Richards at all."[211] Maybe in the Field of Dreams he will learn how to express his affection to those important to him.

Fittingly, he died on the golf course, found slumped in his golf cart after he had finished his round.

[209] Brad Synder, *A Well-Paid Slave: Curt Flood's Fight for Free Agency in Professional Sports.* Viking, 2006, 123.

[210] Cited in Corbett, 384.

[211] Cited in Corbett, 385.

Fred "Dixie" Walker
1910-1982
Career: 1933-1949; Mgr./Coach/Scout: 1951-1970

Fred "Dixie" Walker was an outfielder who spent most of his career with the New York Yankees and the Brooklyn Dodgers. Following his playing career he remained with the Dodger organization as a batting instructor and scout, and also later served as a coach in the Braves organization.

A few baseball experts, though not many, believe that Dixie Walker deserves Hall of Fame consideration. His career numbers - 1,905 games, .306 average, 2,064 hits (he won the batting title in 1944 and was RBI leader in 1945) - indicate he was certainly a solid, above average player. And, for his years as a Brooklyn Dodger (1939-1947) he was far and away the most popular player on the team. The Dodger fans loved his drawl, his honesty and his folksiness and referred to him as "The People's Choice" (or "The Peeple's Cherce" in Brooklynese). Although not a Hall of Famer he is included in our study for several reasons.

First, for personal reasons. I was raised in his hometown

of Birmingham, Alabama, and have a first-hand knowledge of the racism that pervaded the city during his lifetime. He is also buried not far from my parents in Elmwood Cemetery in Birmingham.

Second, Walker deserves a lot of credit for initiating the player's pension system that is today one of the most generous in sports. Many modern baseball fans are not aware of the total control that owners had over players for much of the history of the game. Players with either long or short careers had no pension until Walker started the process, finalized in 1947. The plan was improved upon in subsequent years, but Walker spent much time and energy bringing about this revolutionary development in the baseball world.

Thirdly, his name is almost exclusively connected today with the role he supposedly played in the effort by some Dodger players to prevent Jackie Robinson from joining the team in 1947. Walker was widely accused of circulating a petition among southern players which would be presented to owner Branch Rickey. No such petition has ever surfaced, and Walker vigorously denied the charges until his death. What is documented is his letter to Rickey that year asking to be traded, although no reason is cited. Although Walker worked well with black players later as a minor league manager and as an excellent batting instructor, it is safe to say that he was a product of his environment and would be considered a racist by virtually any definition. To his credit, he seemed to have moved beyond his racist views, and after baseball integrated he changed with the times and exhibited rather healthy racial attitudes in the last half of his life. In every public statement from Walker, he had nothing but praise for Robinson as a player and as a person and said openly that integration improved the game. For example, although Walker didn't tend to give rookies any batting tips, he did do this for Jackie not long after Jackie joined the team. In addition, Walker said to a writer that "No other ballplayer on this club with the possible exception of {catcher} Bruce Edwards had done more to put the Dodgers up in the race than Robinson has. He is everything Branch Rickey said he was when he came up from Montreal."[212]

It is unfair to judge Walker solely on this issue, although it was a historic moment in American history as well as in baseball. Probably no player was more of an avowed and unrepentant racist than Ty Cobb, but Cobb is rightly celebrated as one of the very best players to play the game. One doesn't excuse bad attitudes and behaviors, but at least those attitudes should be understood and judged in light of the environment of the times. To some degree it appears Walker took his stance based of how his views would be received in his home city and state where he ran a business and was a highly public and popular figure in Birmingham and in all of Alabama. There is no question that a pro-integration statement by any public figure at that time, especially in the South, would have spelled doom to one's reputation. It would have taken supernatural courage to buck the history and pervasive attitudes of his culture. He clearly regretted what he did and wished he had responded differently.[213]

Fourth, his marriage to New York City native Estelle Shea offers an amazing study in contrasts, which nonetheless resulted in a very happy and fulfilling marriage. Estelle was Irish and from a devout Roman Catholic family. Dixie was a southern bred boy who was nominally Protestant (more on this later). Estelle already had a successful career in New York City when she met Dixie and was ahead of her times regarding the place of women in society. She showed strength of character when she made Dixie choose between her and his mother as to who would run the household in his absence (which, of

---

[212] Cited in Arnold Rampersad, *Jackie Robinson: A Biography*. Alfred A. Knopf, 1997, 186.

[213] For additional candid comments by Walker, see Maury Allen with Susan Walker, *Dixie Walker of the Dodgers*. The University of Alabama Press, 2010, 153, 164.

course, was most of the time since he was a ballplayer). Dixie did the right thing in confronting his mother about the needed change in her attitude and behavior but this, understandably, led to tension between the two women in Dixie's life. Estelle also stood her ground when Dixie objected to Estelle placing their daughter in a private Catholic school without his consent. She prevailed in that argument.

Estelle certainly played the role of the good wife and mother and ran the household, consisting of four children (another child died in infancy), with great efficiency and grace. Dixie was the titular "head of the household" but Estelle, in fact, was the head, and had to be considering the nature of Walker's profession.

In spite of these substantial differences in upbringing, it was apparent to the children and to all who knew them that these two people were deeply in love and enjoyed each other's company immensely. After Dixie became a scout for the Dodgers, he roamed all over the country looking for prospects, and Estelle could have easily remained at home even though the children were all grown and away. Instead, she chose to ride with him in their red van to remote places and take in the scenic wonders of America. While Dixie sat in a press box taking notes and talking to other baseball people, Estelle happily sat in the stands and read a book. Estelle even celebrated their wedding anniversary every year after Dixie died from stomach cancer in 1982. All of this is a pretty impressive testimony to their devotion to each other. Estelle proved her strength as she outlived Dixie by twenty years, and traveled extensively overseas and regularly up to New England to assist with the grandchildren. Fortunately for her, Dixie had become a "baseball lifer" (52 years in the game!) who earned a decent income and had made good investments . One sad aspect of this marriage was that Estelle's Irish Catholic mother refused to even speak to Estelle after she married a southern Protestant, exhibiting an ugly intolerance and prejudice. There is no indication that Estelle allowed this to embitter her.

Dixie and Estelle had the unfortunate experience of outliving two of their five children. A six-month old infant daughter died of pneumonia due to the fact that Estelle had to take the crying child to their basement so Dixie could get the sleep he needed to play. Today's antibiotics would have saved the child. Dixie's daughter Susan said her father never got over the loss of this child. It is not stated, but it is reasonable to assume that Dixie blamed himself, since he was the reason the child had to be moved to a place in the home which was unhealthy for a young baby. Fred Jr. played professional ball for several years, but drowned in Florida while sky diving, and his body was never recovered. It is well known that couples often grieve differently after the death of a child and that a marriage has a greater chance of dissolving following such a tragedy, but Dixie and Estelle weathered the storms and moved forward together.

Dixie didn't really have a childhood, as he had to leave school to support his former major leaguer and alcoholic father and domineering mother. Nonetheless, he grew to be a soft spoken southern gentleman. His relaxed, kind, and pleasant nature made him a much liked player. He is especially honored by many players who credit Dixie for enabling them to become major league hitters. He was a smart ballplayer and knew how to patiently teach the intricate art of hitting to any and all who would listen.

Dixie had a good singing voice and would often join in with other musical types to loosen up the atmosphere in the clubhouse. He made himself available to speak to many civic organizations. A revealing moment occurred in 1941 when 5,000 fans signed a petition to put Walker back into the starting lineup when he had been benched. The Dodgers also held a day in his honor after he was traded to Pittsburgh. He was able to connect with fans like few other players could do.

Dixie's daughter Susan cooperated with Maury Allen in writing the definitive biography of Walker, and offered several interesting insights into the man.

"I have always felt that both he and I were shortchanged out of sharing each other's lives because of his career. He was always very disciplined, hard-working, critical, and focused. My mother was very accepting and loving, so I naturally gravitated toward her. I think about it now and can't believe my mother never told me how well known and successful he was in baseball. . . I now know how hard it was for him to step in and out of our lives. He tried but really did not understand children as he had never really had a childhood of his own. We fished together but I wasn't allowed to talk. He just concentrated on catching the fish. He was as intense about that as he was about most everything else."[214] She regrets that she never really knew him.

Dixie also spent some of his off-season hours hunting, especially with his brother, fellow major leaguer Harry Walker. He was apparently closer emotionally to Harry than to anyone else, with the possible exception of his wife Estelle. He had no other outside hobbies and had no interest in night life.

Religion became a part of Dixie's life only in his later years. Susan noted that Dixie was eventually baptized in a Presbyterian church and concluded that "in his later life my father was just searching for God."[215] But throughout their married life Dixie was supportive of Estelle's devotion to the Catholic church. Dixie even became friendly with a local priest who went so far as to petition the Pope for a dispensation to marry Dixie and Estelle in the church. The request was granted and their marriage ceremony meant that Estelle was no longer excommunicated from the church and could receive the sacraments again. Dixie would often drive Estelle to Sunday morning Mass in their Birmingham suburb and would remain outside in the car reading the paper. And, despite initial resistance to raising the

---

[214]   *Ibid.*, 246.
[215]   *Ibid.*, 248.

children Catholic, Susan believes that Dixie slowly came to appreciate their religious training.

Dixie developed stomach cancer in 1981 and was treated aggressively with chemotherapy. But in early 1982 the cancer had spread to his gall bladder, kidney, and colon, and he was in a great deal of pain. The long illness exhausted the family for many months. He died in St. Vincent's Hospital in Birmingham (where I was born!!) on May 17, 1982.

His funeral service was unpretentious as he had requested. Eddie Stanky and his wife were the only baseball people who attended. Daughter Susan said the service was very dignified and sad.[216]

For trivia buffs, we can note that his first hit was off the premier reliever of his day, Firpo Marberry. And Walker is credited as being the only player in history to catch his own home run. This strange event occurred in Ebbets Field when his home run lodged in the right field screen. After the Dodger half of the inning Walker he took his regular position in right field, shook the ball loose and caught it.

---

[216] *Ibid.*, 256.

Theodore Samuel Williams
1918-2002
Playing Career: 1939-1942; 1946-1960
Managerial career 1969-1972
Nicknames: "The Kid," "The Splendid Splinter"

Ted Williams was an outfielder for the Boston Red Sox. He was elected to the Hall of Fame in 1966.

Named after "Teddy" Roosevelt and called "Teddy" at home, Ted and his brother Danny were the product of an unsupervised home life in San Diego, California. Ted's father Sam was a photographer who left early in the morning and came home late at night and rarely smiled. His mother May was a religious zealot, working virtually all her waking hours for the Salvation Army. The boys often could not enter the home most nights until their mother came home around 10:00. Also, the boys often had to participate in the Salvation Army's activities and both came to resent it. Ted's lifelong rejection and even disgust with religion started in his childhood, likely the result of his mother's neglect of him due to her religious fanaticism, although he did learn how to be generous and charitable from her work with the Salvation Army.

Swearing became an art form for Ted and a way for him to lash out at whatever displeased him. Biographer Leigh Montville notes that Ted's f-bombs and other vile words were usually modified with his favorite adjective, "syphilitic." Furthermore, in his outbursts he could string together words to produce a sort of profane poetry, with a rhythm and cadence to his swearing. "There was a blasphemous direction to much of the anger addressed upward toward a syphilitic Supreme Being who had let humanity down just one more time."[217] In addition, it didn't matter where he was when he would let go with his angry

---

[217] Leigh Montville, *Ted Williams: The Biography of an American Hero.* Broadway Books, 2004, 11.

profanity, since he lacked a "social muffler" that most people have. It didn't seem to matter to Ted what people thought of him.

Ted's view of women provides a thick case study for feminist critique. "Women were a constant problem: a joy, a nuisance, a mystery, a lower life form put on earth mostly to entertain and complain."[218] His three marriages ended in divorce (his most stable relationship seems to have been with a "groupie," Louise Kaufman), and he was not present at the births of his three children. Although alienated from his first child, Bobby Jo, in his later years he became close to his only son, John Henry, and his other daughter, Claudia.

John Henry and Claudia were children from Ted's third marriage. Dolores Wattach was a striking model that Ted met on an overseas flight. She had auditioned for the role of Pussy Galore in the James Bond movie Goldfinger.

In 1969 Dolores agreed to a lengthy interview and she spoke frankly about how difficult it was to be Ted Williams' wife. Her brutally honest statements were like what viewers witness today on programs like Dr. Phil. It is stunning to read her innermost thoughts and feelings. The interviewer, Don Newberry, was due to play the tape on a radio show. But after he played the tape for his wife, she said, "You can't put that on the air." Newberry agreed and placed the tape in a box in his basement where it sat for over thirty years.[219]

In 2014 Claudia wrote *Ted Williams: My Father*, a moving memoir published to offset the wave of negative publicity generated by the accounts of Ted's final months and the decision to place his body in the Alcor Life Extension facility in Scottsdale, Arizona (more on this later).

Although Claudia's affection for her father runs deep, she freely admits that he was a complex human being and hard to figure out, that he was a perfectionist and a control freak,

---

[218] *Ibid.*, 11.
[219] Montville cites the full interview on pp. 279-293.

and that he was disrespectful of and, at times, abusive toward women.[220] Furthermore, she often experienced his intense anger that seemingly exploded out of nowhere. She believed Ted took his anger and hurt to the batter's box, venting his frustrations and anger on a baseball. In addition she concluded that his anger was directed not so much at a person, but at a situation that he couldn't control or resolve. She especially saw his anger towards God when Ted visited sick children in hospitals. "Everyone knew what Ted Williams was mad about. There was no excuse for children to be sick with cancer. Surely someone who could turn water to wine, walk on water, and raise the dead could prevent the cruel disease of cancer from affecting innocent children. It challenged his faith and his willingness to believe in God."[221]

Many observers would assume Williams was an atheist, but it seems more accurate to say that God was present to Ted as an enemy. Sportswriter Russ White said that "God was with him everywhere. God just pissed him off an awful lot. God was often the enemy." Yet White said Williams was one of the most spiritual people he had ever met because he tried hard to live by the Golden Rule, helped the needy, didn't let money become an idol, and possessed real humility beneath all the braggadocio.[222]

In spite of Ted's highly publicized negative attributes, Claudia often saw another side of Ted. He was extremely empathetic and often generous to a fault. His tenderness towards children was not done for public show, but sprang deep from within Ted. He contributed countless hours and substantial monies

---

[220] Claudia Williams, *Ted Williams: My Father.* Harper-Collins, 2014, 9, 34, 42.

[221] *Ibid.*, 165.

[222] Described in Montville, 422.

to promote the Jimmy Fund, a charity set up to assist sick children. Ted was at his best around children in need.[223]

Claudia confessed that she felt compelled to write her memoirs to counter Montville's reliance on several of Ted's caregivers, most of whom were critical of John Henry's handling of Ted's health care and financial affairs. She viewed them as "hangers' on" who violated their confidentiality agreements to put themselves in the limelight and claim to speak on Ted's behalf when they had been around him only short periods of time. She vigorously defends her brother's decisions and care of their father.

Claudia also insists, contrary to statements from those Montville's designated as "sources close to the family" (who were not identified) in the last months of his life, that Ted wholeheartedly agreed with the decision to undergo vitrification, where the body is not "frozen" but cooled to -200 degrees Fahrenheit by liquid nitrogen. She chronicles how Ted, John Henry, and herself talked at length about this procedure, signed a pact in 2000, with the focus on the hope that all three of them would be reunited in the distant future. She also blames Ted's estranged daughter Bobby Jo for much of the furor following Ted's death, which robbed the family of the planned memorial service. Through all of this turmoil Claudia laments that she lost her faith in people.[224]

To add to what reads like a soap opera, John Henry was diagnosed with acute myelogenous leukemia fourteen months after Ted died. An email to John Henry from Bobby Jo read: "I

---

223 Montville chronicles a moving example of Ted's concern for youth in need in the last few years of his life when he met Tricia Miranti during rehabilitation after his first stroke. "Williams gave his failing heart to the teenage Miranti. The sweetest sound became her giggle. He tried hard to bring out that giggle as hard as he could. The sick old ballplayer and the sick kid became fast friends. . .He. . .set up a foundation for her." Montville, 422ff.

224 *Ibid.*, 252, 263, 271, 287, 299ff.

hope you suffer. I hope you die slowly thinking of the pain you put Daddy through – you deserve it." A few months later John Henry joined his father at Alcor.

Ted was widely acclaimed for his military service. He became an accomplished pilot and served in both World War II and in the Korean conflict. His spectacular crash landing of a jet plane in 1953 made him into a folk hero.[225]

Williams was ahead of his time in regard to racial issues. There is no record of any prejudicial words or actions during his entire lifetime. Furthermore, Ted was at the forefront of the move to elect blacks into the Hall of Fame. He made the bold and shocking statement (for that time) that Satchel Paige, Josh Gibson, and others from the old Negro Leagues deserved to be in the Hall during his Hall of Fame speech in 1966 [226] While politically Ted was an outspoken conservative Republican (Hoover was his favorite president), he possessed a social conscience.

One will search in vain to find negative comments about Ted from those who played with him and against him. Numerous players opined about Ted in the huge 1994 volume *We Played the Game* where 65 players who played from 1947-1964 shared their observations about the Golden Era of Baseball. There was unanimous agreement that although Ted was a loner and not easy to get to know, he was an unselfish team leader and teacher, willing to talk to any player, including rookies, about hitting. Teammates felt that he always gave 100% and was usually misunderstood by sportswriters.[227] One of his managers,

---

[225] See the detailed account in Montville, 162-165. For an overall look at Ted's military career, see Bill Nowlin, "Ted Williams at War" in *When Baseball Went to War*. Ed. By Anton, Todd, and Nowlin, Bill. Triumph Books, 2008, 155-160.

[226] Larry Tye, *Satchel: The Life and Times of an American Legend*. Random House, 2009, 268.

[227] Danny Peary (Ed.). *We Played the Game*. Black Dog and Leventhal Publishers, 1994, 163, 236, 413, 203, 411.

Joe McCarthy, had high praise for Ted. "He was in the ball game every day. He played. He hustled. Followed orders. Of course I only gave him one order – hit. No subordination there. He hit."[228]

However, the same praise is rarely found in those he managed in his brief managerial career. His sharp-tongued criticism made him a hard man to play for, even for those who were giving their very best. Yet he was successful in helping some players improve their game and was voted American League Manager-of-the-Year in his first year with the Washington Senators. But it was down hill from that point on.

Williams resented those who viewed him as "a natural hitter." As a perfectionist he spent countless hours working at the craft of hitting. When asked why he was successful, he replied, "Practice, practice, practice." He applied that same work ethic to everything he did. Not only did he want to be remembered as the greatest hitter in the game of baseball, he considered himself to be the greatest fisherman of all time, engaging in his favorite hobby with the same passion and drive seen in his relentless pursuit of hitting mastery.

While speaking of fishing, it is not surprising that Ted's many fishing buddies were ambivalent about their time spent with him fly-fishing. Ted would never fail to criticize his partners, often in harsh language, yet he did indeed teach them a better way to do it.

In writing about the historic 1941 season when Ted hit .406, highly acclaimed sportswriter Robert Creamer waxes eloquently in describing Williams.

"Today we see Williams as a big, handsome man who as he aged grew ruggedly better looking in the true-blue 100% American John Wayne manner, a man engagingly outspoken and opinionated, a charmer. We see him through four decades of baseball. . . (But in 1941) the public considered (him) a

---

[228] Cited in *Red Smith on Baseball*. Ivan R. Dee, 2000, 333.

behavior problem. He dressed oddly, which is to say he wouldn't wear a tie in an era when wearing a tie in public was almost as important as wearing shoes. He had temper tantrums. . .He was impulsive, outspoken and rash. . . He always got along better with what are called little people, particularly blue-collar types, than he did with the more glamorous people who flock like hungry pigeons around baseball stars, and he got along well with the men in his uncle's firehouse. He'd stay there for hours sometime, talking and kidding around. . . The term "flake" had not yet come into vogue, but Williams at the beginning of 1941 was considered a flake – a hell of a hitter, yes, but not yet a real ballplayer."[229]

A different kind of "flake" in Ted's time was the irrepressible "Bobo" Newsom, who pitched for nine teams during his amazing career from 1929-1953. In spite of losing more games than he won (211 wins, 222 losses) and being a pain in the ass to all the teams he played for, he was a huge fan favorite in every city in which he played (even the opposing fans loved him). He brought laughter and entertainment to the game. He also feared no man and didn't hesitate to lecture Ted about Ted's infamous treatment of the fans. Bobo believed that fans deserved respect. Ted was unreceptive and unrepentant, asking Bobo to name any player who had been helped by the popularity stuff. "Brother, you're looking at one right now," replied Bobo. Bobo noted that even though he had had losing seasons the past two years, he had gotten raises both times because the crowd got a kick out of him. Fans laugh, boo, and cheer, but Bobo took it all in stride: "If you only tip your hat to the customers and stop cussing them back there's no telling how great and popular you'd be."[230] But being popular was never

---

[229] Robert W. Creamer, *Baseball in 1941*. Viking, 1991, 14-17.

[230] Jim McConnell, *Bobo Newsom: Baseball's Traveling Man*. McFarland & Co., 2016, 175.

high on Ted's list, so he remained indifferent or dismissive towards fans to the very end.

In the entire history of baseball, Ted Williams ranks high on the list when it comes to describing complex and intriguing personalities. He had inner demons with which to wrestle. He could drive people close to him crazy. At other times, he could charm their socks off. He could be both gracious and cruel, often in extreme ways. He was an amazing ballplayer and an amazing human being.

Carl Furillo
1922-1989
Career: 1946-1960

Carl Anthony Furillo played his entire major league career as a right-fielder (with a few games in center and left) for the Brooklyn/Los Angeles Dodgers. Born to a typical rural Italian family near Reading, Pennsylvania, his strong throwing arm earned him the moniker "The Reading Rifle." Another nickname given by his Italian buddies was "Skoonj," an Italian word for snail.

Carl Furillo could properly fit into several of the categories of our study. To those who knew him well he was a really good guy. There was also a tragic aspect of his story. When he was released by the Dodgers in 1960, he became bitter toward the Dodgers and toward baseball in general. This bitterness persisted for decades, until it was partially mitigated only a few years before his death.

It's easy to harbor some mixed feelings about Furillo,

primarily due to his stubbornness, which made his retirement from baseball much worse than it had to be. When he was released in 1960, he made up his mind that he had been treated unjustly by the Dodgers, and genuine efforts by the Dodger management to deal with the problems were explicitly dismissed by Furillo. In reading the largely sympathetic account of the matter by Furillo's biographer, Ted Reed[231], one is left with the impression that Furillo shares a great deal of the blame for refusing to sit down and work out a solution. Instead, he filed suit against the Dodgers, which guaranteed an amicable resolution to the issue would not be forthcoming. Furillo's combative style, which served him well on the diamond, failed him in negotiation with the Dodgers on how to end his playing career.

Although understandable for one who completed only an 8th grade education and who possessed no marketable skills outside of baseball, Furillo's preoccupation with money leaves a negative impression about him. Even taking into account his Depression-era upbringing and the sad fact that players of his day were not compensated fairly by the owners, Furillo's tendency to view everything through the prism of money projects a less than balanced perspective on life.

On the plus side, though, Furillo was a hard worker his entire life, and made wise investments insuring him of a comfortable retirement. After baseball he worked at several blue-collar jobs and always gave his best to every employer. Many players of his era never came close to Furillo's level of financial security. He earned everything he owned, and he was a good steward of his resources.

Furillo personified the positive stereotypical Italian prominence of family. He was devoted to his wife Fern and to

---

[231] Ted Reed, *Carl Furillo: Brooklyn Dodgers All-Star.* McFarland & Co., 2011. Most of the information about Furillo is culled from this excellent biography.

his children. He took them to spring training, and during the off season, unlike Mickey Mantle, he would remain at home engaging in activities with his wife and children. He didn't carouse like a number of those in our study, but instead devoted his free time to his loved ones. There is little indication that his sense of moral obligation to others extended beyond his larger family. For him, to be moral was to work hard and provide for his family.

Furillo's well-deserved tough guy image made it hard for him to exude warmth toward others. He would freely dispense advice and respect to others, but he seemed unable to connect emotionally to most others outside his family. Outside of the home, everything was cold-hearted business and should be handled accordingly. He was so private in his personal life that he wouldn't share the fact that his father's serious illness occupied much of his free time from 1950 to 1951. His playing prowess tailed off due to the frequent visits to see his dying father, but he wouldn't tell anyone because he didn't want to appear he was making excuses for his problems on the field. Later, he also didn't share with others that he was suffering from leukemia. Old colleagues didn't understand why he didn't participate in activities that seemed a natural fit for him. For Carl, personal issues were strictly personal. However, when refusal to share important personal information affects one's relationships with significant others, it would seem that privacy issues merit another look. Here Furillo's well-known hard headedness prevented him from revisiting matters that he deemed settled.

Like many who fought in World War II, Furillo was hesitant to share his experiences on the battlefield. He saw action in Guam and Okinawa and was cited for bravery. In keeping with his nature, he was offered a Purple Heart due to a minor battle wound but turned down the honor, feeling he didn't deserve it. His experience in seeing the carnage made him withdraw even more into himself, not wanting to talk about the horror of warfare.

Clearly Furillo's exit from the game and his reaction to it was a defining moment in his life. His perspective of what happened set the tone for most of the remaining years of his life. There remained a bitterness in him that wasn't healthy for his psyche and for his dealings with those outside the circle of his family. There is a sadness here that didn't need to be.

Another unfortunate defining moment for Furillo had to do with the arrival in 1947 of Jackie Robinson, one of the key events in the history of baseball. The film version of *The Jackie Robinson Story* placed Furillo in an unfavorable light which he was never able to shake. Although Furillo freely admitted that he wasn't keen on integrating blacks into baseball, he is unfairly singled out when most white players of his day weren't happy about this radically new development in baseball. The fact is that Furillo quickly accepted Jackie's presence on the team and slowly became a good friend to the Robinsons. One has to remember that Jackie's combative nature, combined with the extreme hostility he faced everywhere he went, made it hard for most others to relate to him during those tumultuous early years of integration when Jackie seemed to have a chip on his shoulder. Easy going personalities like Roy Campanella had an easier time connecting with others and letting those nasty racial comments roll off like water from a duck's back. So, it is to Furillo's credit that he worked on his attitude toward integration and eventually became fully accepting of blacks on his team.

Carl seemed to mellow in the last decade of his life. He was approachable to all on his last job as a security guard at a nearby plant, welcoming his celebrity status in the company. He also enjoyed attending card signing events and visiting with baseball fans.

His final years were spent hunting, fishing and gardening. He finally seemed to be at peace with the Dodgers, although it is clear that there remained some lingering bitterness that he couldn't quite jettison.

Suffering from congestive heart failure he died in his sleep of a massive heart attack on January 21, 1989. His funeral was delayed allowing visitors from around the country to attend. Several teammates, including Carl Erskine, Joe Black, Sandy Koufax, Clem Labine, and Johnny Podres, as well as Dodger owner Peter O'Malley, attended the service. After the service, O'Malley offered to pay for the funeral, but wife Fern declined. Erskine delivered a moving eulogy, pointing out that the tough, strong-willed Furillo also possessed a sensitive and tender side as well. All those who played and worked with him respected the man, and most expressed affection for him. But he was not someone you could mess with. He was a tough cookie. Fern told him in the midst of difficult situations, "Dago, stick to your guns." He certainly did that.

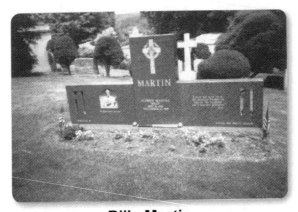

Billy Martin
1928-1989
Career: Player: 1950-61; Mgr.: 1969-88

Billy Martin played second base for the New York Yankees and several other teams before achieving most of his notoriety as manager of the Yankees and several other teams.

Like Ty Cobb before him, Billy Martin was combative and pugnacious as a result of both nature and nurture. His naturally fiery personality was reinforced primarily by his little 4'11' ninety-five-pound Italian mother Jennie Downey. One of Billy's indelible memories was when his mother tried to attack a 6'4" teacher who she felt had physically punished Billy unjustly. She yelled: "If you ever lay your hands on my son again, I'll come up here and break every bone in your body!" On another occasion when a policeman manhandled Billy, she told him, "If you every put your hands on him again, I'll beat the living shit out of you!" This mother could intimidate anybody, and she always stood up for her children. On yet another occasion, a neighbor, a World War I veteran, was picking on Billy and she proceeded to attack the man with both fists. Billy remembers, "she beat the hell out of him, and Mom didn't get a scratch."[232] Billy's Mom taught him to "never take shit off of nobody," and it is safe to say that Billy

---

[232] These incidents are taken from Billy Martin & Pete Golenbock, *Number One*. Delacorte Press, 1980, 29f.

followed this parental advice to the letter. According to Mickey Mantle when Billy and his mother were together, they argued constantly and cussed each other. She once hit Billy with a frying pan during a dinner argument.[233]

Billy, born and raised in Berkeley, California, was named after his father Alfred Manuel Martin, the second of his mom's husbands. Alfred was a Portuguese musician from Hawaii to whom his mom was married to for less than a year. When he showed up one day when Billy was fifteen, Billy told him to get lost. He had virtually no contact with him for the rest of his life. Interestingly, Billy didn't know his real name until junior high school, when waiting to be assigned to a home room, he didn't respond to the called name of Alfred Manuel Martin. When he told the teacher that she hadn't called his name, she informed him of his legal name. The name "Billy" came from his grandmother, who spoke only Italian, who called him "Bellitz," which means "beautiful." Everyone thought she was saying "Billy" and that is what everyone called him.

Billy was especially angry when called a "bastard," since his father was not around, as well as when called "wop" or "dago." Bigger boys liked to pick on him because he was small with big ears and a big nose. Fights were common, and the fact was that Billy, although only 5'10" and never more than 160 pounds, could hit like a heavyweight. He regularly knocked out guys much bigger than he. In fact, some claim that Billy would have made an excellent prize fighter because he had quick hands and could hit hard. He was rightly called "The Graziano of Baseball."

While growing up he headed a gang of toughs in Berkerley who would go to bars and beat up people for the fun of it. They also liked to beat up college kids at UCal, as well as start fights with servicemen outside theaters.

---

[233] Pete Golenbock, *Seven: The Mickey Mantle Novel.* The Lyons Press, 2007, 93.

Billy claimed that he never started a fight, but he certainly seemed to invite them. He carried his fighting skills into the majors where he had several celebrated fights. He once had a fight with Jimmy Piersall, who was then sent to the minors where he suffered a nervous breakdown. Even the tough Billy felt bad about this. That same year he decked Clint "Scrap Iron" Courtney, who Satchel Paige said was "the meanest man I ever met."[234] It would not be the last time he and Courtney traded punches. One time he sucker-punched Chicago pitcher Jim Brewer and broke his cheekbone. When Billy learned that Brewer was suing him for a million dollars, Billy asked, "How does he want it, cash or check?" He beat up the traveling secretaries of both the Twins and the Rangers. He gave a fat lip to a marshmallow salesman and knocked out cold his twenty-game winner Dave Boswell, who suffered a black eye, chipped tooth, and twenty stitches on his face. He fared less well in 1987 with Ed Whitson, who broke Billy's arm and bruised his side. He was also badly beaten in a Texas topless bar in 1988.[235] In sum, Billy was "a tightly wound box of noise. Wherever he goes you have a racket. You don't look for Martin. You listen for him."[236] Or as his contemporary, George Kell, observed, "There was no

---

[234] Floyd Conner, *Baseball's Most Wanted*. Galahad Press, 2000, 294.

[235] All of these fights are listed in Conner, 293f. Bert Sugar lists the dates and combatants of the nineteen known fights in Billy's career in Bert Sugar, ed. *The Baseball Maniac's Almanac*, 2nd Edition. Skyhorse Publishing, 2010, 216. See also Jason Turbow with Michael Duca, *The Baseball Codes: Beanballs, Sign Stealing & Bench-Clearing Brawls: The Unwritten Rules of America's Pastime*. Pantheon Books, 2010, 149, for the story of how Billy sucker-punched pitcher Jim Brewer on the mound, knocking him out cold.

[236] Gene Schoor, *Billy Martin: The Story of Baseball's Unpredictable Genius*. Doubleday & Co., 1980, 120.

one better ...to light a four-alarm fire than Billy Martin. When it came to creating excitement, he was a legitimate arsonist."[237]

Reds pitcher Jim O'Toole said that Martin had a Napoleon complex many little guys have and always seemed to be in a fight, although he got along well with everyone on the team.[238] Ewell Blackwell echoed this observation, noting that he would fight at the drop of a hat, but only with members of the other teams.[239] White Sox player Jim Landis observed that Billy was sneaky in that he would instigate a brawl and then often back away and let others fight.[240]

Billy was a good ballplayer, but certainly not in the category of such Yankee greats like Babe Ruth, Joe DiMaggio, and Mickey Mantle. He made his mark as a manager, and he was a good one. He taught the fundamentals of the game, developed brilliant strategies, and generally managed his players well, making sure not to criticize them in front of other players. His infamous near fight in the dugout with Reggie Jackson was an exception. To manage as well as he did under George Steinbrenner, "the boss from hell," is remarkable.

Like many ballplayers of his time, Billy loved to drink, beginning in high school, and his love of booze only increased as the years went by. Some around him would maintain that he became an alcoholic. Of course, Billy denied it. One thing is certain: bad things seemed to happen when he drank a lot. In his defense, Billy was probably right when he insisted that it was and is common for guys in bars to pick fights with athletes. Drinking convinces some men that they can whip anybody, and

[237] George Kell with Dan Ewald, *Hello Everybody, I'm George Kell*. Sports Publishing, 1998, 146. Kell acknowledged that Billy was an outstanding field manager. "The problem was Billy could never manage himself. He couldn't handle his personal problems," 95.

[238] Danny Peary (ed), *We Played the Game*. Black Dog and Leventhal, 1994, 476.

[239] *Ibid.*, 209.

[240] *Ibid.*, 379.

it would be a special bragging point to duke it out with a well-known athlete. Having said that, Billy found it hard to walk away from a challenge when it would have been in his best interest to do so. Many of these confrontations ended up in court, and likely led to his being fired a time or two. It should come as no surprise that Billy's premature death was a result of drinking and driving.

Billy, like Cobb, could intimidate an entire team, believing that you could often win a game before it started. As a player Billy would swagger, spike fielders when sliding into bases, tag players hard on the head, trip runners, etc. Casey Stengel liked this about Billy, who mirrored Casey's hard playing and willingness to do whatever was needed to win. With Casey's encouragement Billy became a first-rate bench jockey. Cleveland General Manager Frank Lane said that Billy was the kind of guy you'd like to kill on the other team, but you wanted to have ten like him on your own team.[241]

Casey became the father that Billy never had. Like many managers Casey tried not to become attached to players because it would become difficult to get rid of a player who is no longer any use to the team. But in Billy's case, Casey couldn't help himself. Casey just loved everything about "Billy the Kid," even though Billy was the only player who would argue with "The Perfesser." Casey had the insight to see that Billy had a deep-rooted insecurity, and he knew how to handle Billy. In spite of this close relationship, when Casey traded him to Kansas City Billy wouldn't speak to Casey for six years.

As a Yankee player Billy was not only the leader on the field, essentially becoming a manager on the field, but became the leader of the "Three Musketeers" with Mickey Mantle and Whitey Ford. The three of them would go out to bars following the game and enjoy the drinking and the comradery, but, of course, these forays often led to problems. Billy was like a big

---

[241] Schoor, 1.

brother to Mickey, who followed Billy around like an adoring kid and did whatever Billy told him to do The Yankee brass wanted to get rid of Billy because he was said to be a bad influence on Mickey and several other players. Phil Rizzuto responded to this allegation saying: "He (Martin) roomed with me in 1950, and I won the Most Valuable Player award. He roomed with Yogi for a year and Yogi was MVP. Then he roomed with Mickey, and Mickey won the MVP *both* years. If that's a bad influence, then the Yankees should have spread it around, and had Billy roomed with a different guy every year."[242] Billy and Mickey also spent many hours together in the off-season as well, as Billy would drop in at Mickey's house unannounced and stay for weeks while they went hunting and fishing along with their night drinking bouts.

For some reason Billy was the only player that the great Joe DiMaggio related to. Maybe it was because both were Italians from the San Francisco area. But it was also because Billy wasn't intimidated by the Clipper and would even tease the stoic loner. Billy would often walk behind Joe in the clubhouse, mimicking the way Joe walked, much to the delight of the players. Even Joe would laugh while still calling Billy "You fresh little bastard." To everyone's amazement Billy was the only one with whom Joe would sit and talk for hours while nursing a beer.[243] Apparently, Billy's cordial, unpretentious nature put Joe at ease. Billy once made a remark about Yogi that he probably thought was a compliment,but didn't come across that way. Billy said that Yogi was a great coach but couldn't be a manager because he wasn't mean enough. To which Jim Bouton responded: "Crap. How many pennants did Bill win for being so mean? Two? That's what Yogi won by not

---

[242] Cited in Allen Barra, *Yogi Berra: Eternal Yankee*. W.W. Norton, 2009, 239.

[243] Tony Castro, *Mickey Mantle: America's Prodigal Son*. Brassey, 2002, 102f.

being mean."[244] Surprisingly, with all the celebrated tirades and meltdowns with umpires, Billy is only 14th on the list of game ejections, with forty-five early showers in 2,267 games.[245]

Billy's relationship with women was something else. His idea of a perfect relationship was to get a woman drunk, make out with her for an hour or two, then get out the door and get ready for the next one.[246] He and Mantle would often have bets about which woman they could seduce. They even went so far as to place a bet on who could make out with the ugliest woman on any given evening. They would often swap "dates" during the night.

It is therefore not surprising that Martin, a genuine male chauvinist, had a hard time maintaining a marriage. He first married Lois Berndt when he was twenty-two. He fought the divorce several years later but Lois hit the nail on the head when she said that "You can't stay in love with a newspaper clipping, not for long, not forever."[247] Billy was restless and never wanted to stay at home. At one time Billy essentially had two wives, keeping a house with one in Oakland and another in Los Angeles without the two knowing about the other.

There was a tender side to this pugnacious fighter who attended Mass regularly at St. Patrick's when he lived in New York City. Those close to him experienced love, loyalty, and humility, which those on the outside never saw. There was this warm, religious, and sentimental side that is hard to explain. Once, when teammate Phil Rizzuto received a death threat

---

[244] Cited in Barra, 307.

[245] Josh Pahigian, *The Seventh Inning Stretch: Baseball's Most Essential and Inane Debates.* Lyons Press, 2010, 41. For the record the top ten are: (through 2008) Bobby Cox, John McGraw, Earl Weaver, Leo Durocher, Frankie Frisch, Paul Richards, Tony LaRussa, Joe Torre, Lou Piniella, and Clark Griffith.

[246] Golenbock, *Seven*, 110.

[247] Cited in Schoor, 62.

letter from a crazy Red Sox fan, Billy traded uniforms with Rizzuto, apparently willing to take a bullet for his teammate.[248]

As every baseball fan knows, Billy's relationship with Yankee owner George Steinbrenner was the stuff of legends. Steinbrenner was a sadist and Martin a masochist, so they were made for each other. Following the last firing Billy and friend Bill Reedy had gone out to a local bar and on the way home Billy was driving and got within a hundred feet of his house when he crashed his truck into a culvert and was killed. Reedy, who was injured badly, placed himself in the driver's seat, fearing that if Billy got a DWI he wouldn't be hired again, but he didn't know that the crash had broken Billy's neck. Billy was sixty-one years old.

An astounding 6,500 showed up for Billy's funeral at St. Patrick's Cathedral. About 3000 jammed into the sanctuary, many of whom had to stand. Mourners included former President Richard Nixon and well- known players such as Mickey Mantle, Whitey Ford, Yogi Berra, Phil Rizutto as well as numerous other ball players and baseball officials (including Steinbrenner).[249]

Billy wanted to be buried in Berkeley next to his mother, but since Jill hated Billy's family, she wouldn't allow it. Ironically, Steinbrenner had him buried in the Gate of Heaven cemetery north of New York City, not far from the Babe's burial site.

Billy's wife Jill distributed Billy's estate, which was worth quite a bit. She gave Billy's two kids $8.82 each and squandered the rest, according to Mickey.[250] Only a day after the funeral the IRS filled three liens against Martin's estate to recover $86,137 in back taxes, claiming that Martin had under-reported income for the years 1981, 1982, and 1988. It seems ole Billy could cause a ruckus even after his death.

[248] *Ibid.*, 6.
[249] Murray Chass, "Mourners Pack Cathedral for Martin's Funeral," *New York Times*, December 30, 1989.
[250] Golenbock, *Seven*, 264.

APPENDIX I

THE DEATH OF RAY CHAPMAN

August 16, 2020, marked the one hundredth anniversary of one of the saddest days in baseball history. Cleveland Indians shortstop Ray Chapman was hit in the head by a pitch thrown by submarine Yankee pitcher Carl Mays. Following emergency brain surgery, the twenty-nine year old Chapman died the following morning. To this day he is the only major league ballplayer to die as a result of action during a ball game. This tragedy had a profound effect on many lives.

In a fierce battle for the American League pennant, the Yankees were hosting the Indians at the Polo Grounds, the diamond they shared with the New York Giants prior to the construction of Yankee Stadium.

The two main figures in this drama were about as different as any two men could be. Chapman's brief distinguished career had earned him the respect and affection of his teammates and fans throughout the league. He always had a smile on his face. "Chappie," as he was called, had reached stardom in 1917, and had the good fortune to meet the beautiful and talented, and even athletic (an accomplished ice skater), Kathleen Daly, the daughter of one of the richest men in Cleveland. Married in 1919, Chapman, following the advice of his father-in-law, announced that the 1920 season was to be his last. He looked forward to being a part of Martin Daly's thriving business. In spite of being born and raised in poor surroundings in Kentucky, when couples from such widely different social classes rarely married, Chapman charmed the Daly family with his fine singing voice and his delightful story telling. It was said that he brought to the Daly household "the playhouse of the locker room without the coarseness." His best man had been Hubbard, Texas native Tris Speaker, the future Hall of Famer and Chapman's best friend.

Carl Mays, on the other hand, was vilified by his opponents and despised by his teammates. F.C. Lane, a baseball writer as this time, said that this strange and cynical figure had aroused more ill-will and resentment than any other ballplayer on record. He was highly intelligent and above reproach in his personal habits, yet he was lonely and friendless among ballplayers. He was simply an enigma to all who knew him.

On this fateful day Mays, as was his usual custom on days

he pitched, put a chicken neck from the ice box in his pocket that he used throughout the game to keep his mouth moist. Knowing that Chapman was the best bunter in the league, he wanted to pitch him high and tight. In fact, most batters felt that he pitched them too far on the inside of the plate and wasn't averse to throwing directly at them at times.

In a light rain, Chapman led off the 5th inning. Mays' unusual side-arming style made it hard for batters to pick up the ball, and as it sailed toward Chapman's head he made no effort to get out of the way. The sound of the ball hitting Chapman in his left temple was heard throughout the park. It actually sounded like a batted ball before it bounced toward the mound. Mays, thinking that the ball had hit Chapman's bat handle, picked up the ball and threw to first base. Catcher Matty Ruel knew that Chapman was hit and sought to catch him as he sunk to the ground. Chapman was stunned, but still conscious, and tried to speak, but no words came out. He was bleeding from his left ear. While Chapman was on the ground Mays was arguing with the umpire, claiming that the ball hit Chapman's bat. Later Mays tarried to blame the umpire for not throwing out the ball after the first pitch because it had a scuff mark and was wet. Mays was making a bad situation worse. Chapman arose and refused help as he made his way to the centerfield clubhouse, but began to collapse as he reached second base and was then grabbed by two teammates and carried to the clubhouse. He was able to whisper and asked that his wife in Cleveland not be notified yet, and then he asked his trainer, who kept Chapman's wedding ring in his pocket, to place the ring on his finger. Those were his last words. He was rushed to nearby St. Lawrence Hospital. His heart rate fell to forty beats a minute but went back to ninety following surgery. The surgeons told Speaker and the other teammate present to leave as it looked like Chapman was improving. However, he died at 4:45 a.m. Speaker broke the news to Kathleen, pregnant with child, when she arrived via train from Cleveland. She fainted on the spot.

What followed was a sad mess. The Roman Catholic Daly family announced that Chapman had converted to Catholicism and insisted on a Catholic service and burial. Teammates and close friends, Jack Graney and Steve O'Neill, both Catholics, agreed with the Dalys. Speaker, a Protestant, vehemently denied this assertion as did Chapman's parents. When Speaker and Graney were conspicuously absent from the funeral at St. John's Roman Catholic Church, it was reported that both men were so upset over Chapman's death that attendance was impossible. It was reported by another source that Speaker had suffered a nervous breakdown and confined to bed. But a common belief among teammates was that there was a big fight between Speaker against both Graney and O'Neill, and that Speaker refused to attend a Catholic service. (An interesting irony: Speaker later married a Catholic!) Speaker somehow convinced the Daly family to bury Chapman in the Protestant Lakeview Cemetery instead of in the Daly family plot at Calvary Cemetery.

The tragedy continued. Kathleen went into a deep depression from which she never recovered. She cut off virtually all outside contacts and rarely left her home. The Chapman child, Rae Marie, essentially suffered the loss of both parents. Kathleen remarried two years later to a cousin. Her sudden death in 1928 proved to be controversial. The family said that she poisoned herself when she accidently mistook a bottle of cleaning fluid or some other substance for her medication to treat depression. However, the Cleveland newspapers attributed her death to "self-administered poisonous acid." A copy of the coroner's report sent to Chapman's mother also listed the cause of death as suicide.

Then, to top it all, Rae Marie died less than a year later at age eight after contracting measles.

Of course, the tragedy followed Mays to his dying day. Immediately after Chapman's death there were calls from several teams to boycott Mays or have him banned from baseball. Mays received numerous death threats. However, he went on to become an outstanding pitcher. He was never seriously considered for the Hall of Fame, although his numbers were better than those of Waite Hoyt and Herb Pennock, two of Mays' Yankee teammates who were voted into the Hall. It is surmised that, in addition to the beaning of Chapman and Mays strong unpopularity, an accusation that Mays accepted a large amount of money to discreetly lose any close game he was involved in during the 1921 World Series destroyed any chance of admission to the Hall of Fame. Mays denied it and the accusation was never proven. Furthermore, although Mays later earned a fortune, he lost it all in the Wall Street crash. In addition, his wife died, leaving him to raise two children, ages twelve and seven. He later remarried. He recovered financially by scouting for several teams and running a successful fishing resort in Oregon. He conducted baseball camps and stayed connected with the game throughout his long life. He willingly answered inquiries about the Chapman incident, insisting that he did not intentionally throw at Chapman, and that his conscience was clear.

APPENDIX II

GRAVESITE LOCATIONS

Richie Ashburn: Gladwyne United Methodist Church, Gladwyne, PA

Yogi Berra: Gate of Heaven Cemetery, East Hanover, NJ

Roy Campanella: Cremated, Ashes location unknown

Hugh Casey: Mt. Paran Baptist Church Cemetery, Atlanta (Buckhead), GA

Ray Chapman: Lakeview Cemetery, Cleveland, OH

Hal Chase: Oak Hill Memorial Park, San Jose, CA

Curt Flood: Inglewood Park, Inglewood, CA

Carl Furillo: Forest Hills Memorial Park, Reiffton, PA

Gil Hodges: Holy Cross Cemetery, Brooklyn, NY

Harry Hooper: Our Lady of Mt. Carmel Cemetery, Aptos Cemetery, Aptos, CA

Joe Jackson: Woodlawn Memorial Park, Greenville, SC

Addie Joss: Woodlawn Cemetery, Toledo, OH

Willie Keeler: Calvary Cemetery, Queens, NY

Johnny Kling: Mt. Moriah Cemetery, Kansas City, MO

Kenesaw Mountain Landis: Oak Woods Cemetery, Chicago, IL

Al Lopez: Garden of Memories Cemetery, Tampa, FL

Roger Maris: Holy Cross Cemetery, Fargo, ND

Billy Martin: Gate of Heaven Cemetery, Hawthorne, NY

Pepper Martin: Memorial Park, Oklahoma City, OK

Stan Musial: Forever Bellerine Cemetery, Hiram Park Cemetery, Creve Coeur, MO

Lefty O'Doul: Cypress Lawn Memorial, Colma, CA

Herb Pennock: Union Hill Cemetery, Kennett Square, PA

Paul Richards: Hillcrest Park Cemetery, Waxahachie, TX

Dixie Walker: Elmwood Cemetery, Birmingham, AL

Ted Williams: Alcor Life Extension Facility, Scottsdale, AZ

Ross Youngs: Mission Burial Park South, San Antonio, TX

BIBLIOGRAPHY

Aaron, Hank with Lonnie Wheeler. *I Had a Hammer: The Hank Aaron Story*. New York: HarperCollins, 1991.

Alexander, Charles. *John McGraw*. Lincoln: The University of Nebraska Press, 1988.

Allen, Maury with Susan Walker. *Dixie Walker of the Dodgers*. Tuscaloosa, AL: The University of Alabama Press, 2010.

Amoruso, Marino. *Gil Hodges: The Quiet Man*. Middlebury, VT.: Paul S. Eriksson, 1991.

Anton, Todd, and Nowlin, Bill, eds. *When Baseball Went to War*. ???Triumph Books, 2008.

Barra, Allen. *Yogi Berra: Eternal Yankee*. New York: W.W. Norton, 2009.

Barthel, Thomas. *Pepper Martin: A Baseball Biography*. Jefferson, N.C.: McFarland & Co., 2003.

Bogen, Gil. *Johnny Kling: A Baseball Biography*. Jefferson, N.C. 2006.

Brosnan, Jim. *The Long Season*. Chicago: Ivan R. Dee, 2002.

Browning, Reed. *Cy Young: A Baseball Life*. Amherst: The University of Massachusetts Press, 2000.

Castro, Tony. *Mickey Mantle: America's Prodigal Son.* Dulles, VA., 2002.

Cataneo, David. *Casey Stengel: Baseball's "Old Professor."* Nashville, TN, 2003.

Clavin, Tom and Peary, Danny. *Gil Hodges: The Brooklyn Bums, The Miracle Mets, and the Extraordinary Life of a Baseball Legend.* New York: New American Library, 2013.

Clavin, Tom and Peary, Danny. *Roger Maris: Baseball's Reluctant Hero.* New York: Simon & Schuster, 2010.

Conner, Floyd. *Baseball's Most Wanted: The Top Ten of the National Pastime's Outrageous Offenders, Lucky Bounces, and Other Oddities.* Edison, NJ: Galahad Press, 2004.

Cook, William A. *Waite Hoyt: A Biography of the Yankees' Schoolboy Wonder.* Jefferson, N.C., 2004.

Corbett, Warren. *The Wizard of Waxahachie: Paul Richards and the End of Baseball as We Knew It.* Dallas: Southern Methodist University Press, 2009.

Craig, Keith. *Herb Pennock: Baseball's Faultless Pitcher.* New York: Rowman & Littlefield, 2016.

Creamer, Robert W. *Baseball in 1941.* New York: Viking, 1991.

Fleitz, David. *Shoeless: The Life and Times of Joe Jackson.* Jefferson, N.C. McFarland & Co., 2001.

Flood, Curt. *The Way It Is.* New York: Trident, 1971.

Frommer, Harvey. *Shoeless Joe and Ragtime Baseball.* Guilford, Conn.: First Taylor Trade paperback edition, 2017.

Garagiola, Joe. *It's Anybody's Ballgame.* Chicago: Contemporary Books, 1988.

Golenbock, Peter. *Number One.* New York: Delacorte Press, 1980.

Golenbock, Peter. *The Mickey Mantle Novel.* Guilford, Conn: The Lyons Press, 2007.

Gollenback, Peter. *Bums: An Oral History of the Brooklyn Dodgers.* Chicago: Contemporary Books, 2000.

Graham, Frank. *The New York Yankees: An Informal History.* Carbondale: Southern Illinois Press, 1943.

Gropman, Donald. *Say It Ain't So, Joe!: The True Story of Shoeless Joe Jackson and the 1919 World Series.* New York: Lynx Books, 1970.

Heidenry, John. *The Gashouse Gang.* New York: Public Affairs, 2007.

Hirsch, James S. *Willie Mays: The Life, the Legend.* New York: Scribner, 2010.

Hoenig, Donald. *Baseball When the Grass Was Real: Baseball from the Twenties to the Forties, Told by the Men Who Played It.* New York: Coward, McCann & Geoghegan, 1975.

James, Bill. *The New Bill James Historical Baseball Abstract.* New York: Free Press, 2001.

Johnson, Harold, ed. *Who's Who in Major League Baseball.* Chicago: Buxton Publishing Press, 1933.

Jones, David, ed. *Deadball Stars of the American League.* Dulles, VA.: Potomac, 2006.

Kell, George with Dan Ewald. *Hello Everybody: I'm George Kell.* Champaign, Ill: Sports Publishing, 1998.

King, David. *Ross Youngs: In Search of a San Antonio Baseball Legend.* Charleston, S,C.: History Press, 2013.

Kohout, Donell. *Hal Chase: The Defiant Life and Turbulent Times of Baseball's Biggest Crook.* Jefferson, N.C.: McFarland & Co., 2001.

Lanctot, Neil. *Campy: The Two Lives of Roy Campanella.* New York: Simon & Schuster Paperbacks, 2011.

Leutzinger, Richard. *Lefty O'Doul: The Legend that Baseball Nearly Forgot.* Carmel, CA: Carmel Bay Publishing Group, 1997.

Longert, Scott. *Addie Joss: King of the Pitchers.* Cleveland, OH.: SABR, 1998.

Montville, Leigh. *Ted Williams: The Biography of an American Hero.* New York: Broadway Books, 2004.

Montville, Leigh. *The Big Bam.* New York: Doubleday, 2006.

Murphy, Cait. *Crazy '08: How a Cast of Cranks, Boneheads, and Magnates Crated the Greatest Year in Baseball History.* New York: Smithsonian Books, 2007.

Neyer, Rob and Epstein, Eddie. *Baseball Dynasties: The Greatest Teams of All Time.* New York: W.W. Norton, 2000.

Pahigian, Josh. *The Seventh Inning Stretch: Baseball's Most Essential and Inane Debates.* Guilford, Conn: The Lyons Press, 2010.

Peary, Danny, ed. *We Played the Game.* New York: Black Dog and Leventhal Publishers, 1994.

Pietrusza, David. *Judge and Jury: The Life and Times of Judge Kenesaw Mountain Landis.* South Bend, IN: Diamond Communications, 1998.

Rampersad, Arnold. *Jackie Robinson: A Biography.* New York: Alfred A. Knopf, 1997.

Ratajczak, Kenneth J. *The Wrong Man Out.* Bloomington, Ind.: Author House, 2008.

Reed, Ted. *Carl Furillo: Brooklyn Dodgers All-Star.* Jefferson, N.C.: McFarland & Co., 2011.

Ritter, Lawrence. *The Glory of Their Times.* New York: MacMillan, 1966.

Roberts, Robin with Rogers, C. Paul. *My Life in Baseball.* Chicago: Triumph Books, 2003.

Schoor, Gene. *Billy Martin: The Story of Baseball's Unpredictable Genius.* New York: Doubleday & Co., 1980.

Singletary, Wes. *Al Lopez: The Life of Baseball's El Senor.* Jefferson, N.C.: McFarland & Co., 1999.

Snider, Duke with Gilbert, Bill. The Duke of Flatbush. New York: Zebra Books, 1998.

Snyder, Brad. *A Well-Paid Slave: Curt Flood's Fight for Free Agency in Professional Sports.* New York: Viking, 2006.

Spatz, Lyle and Steinberg, Steve. *1921: The Yankees, the Giants, and the Battle for Baseball Supremacy in New York.* Lincoln: University of Nebraska Press, 2010.

Spatz, Lyle. *Willie Keeler: From the Playgrounds of Brooklyn to the Hall of Fame.* New York: Rowman & Littlefield, 2015.

Spatz, Lyle. *Hugh Casey: The Triumphs and Tragedies of a Brooklyn Dodger.* New York: Rowman & Littlefield, 2016.

Sugar, Bert, ed. *The Baseball Maniac's Almanac, 2nd Edition.* New York: Skyhorse Publishing, 2010.

Thomas, Henry W. *Walter Johnson: Baseball's Big Train.* Lincoln: The University of Nebraska Press, 1995.

Turbow, Jason with Duca, Michael. *The Baseball Codes: Beanballs, Sign Stealing & Bench-Clearing Brawls: The Unwritten Rules of America's Pastime.* New York: Pantheon Books, 2010.

Tye, Larry. *Satchel: The Life and Times of an American Legend.* New York: Random House, 2009.

Vescey, George. *Stan Musial: An American Life.* New York: Ballantine Books, 2011.

Vincent, Fay. *We Would Have Played for Nothing: Baseball Stars of the 1950s and 1960s Talk About the Game They Loved.* New York: Simon & Schuster, 2008.

Weeks, Jonathan. *Baseball's Most Notorious Personalities: A Gallery of Rogues.* Lanham, MD: Scarecrow, 2013.

Williams, Claudia. *Ted Williams: My Father.* New York: Harper-Collins, 2014.

Williams, Peter. *When the Giants Were Giants: Bill Terry and the Golden Age of New York Baseball.* Chapel Hill, N.C. : Algonquin Books, 1994.

Wood, John A. *Beyond the Ballpark: The Honorable, Immoral, and Eccentric Lives of Baseball Legends.* New York: Rowman & Littlefield, 1916.

Zimniuch, Fran. *Richie Ashburn Remembered.* Champaign, Ill., 2005.

Zingg, Paul. *Harry Hooper: An American Baseball Life.* Champaign, Ill: University of Illinois Press, 2004.

Printed in the United States
by Baker & Taylor Publisher Services